SHADOW OF PARADISE

VICENTE ALEIXANDRE

SHADOW OF PARADISE

Translated and with an Introduction by
Hugh A. Harter

Foreword by
Claudio Rodríguez

University of California Press
Berkeley and Los Angeles, California
University of California Press, Ltd.
London, England
Spanish text © 1966 by Vicente Aleixandre
English text © 1987 by The Regents of the
University of California
Printed in the United States of America

1 2 3 4 5 6 7 8 9

Library of Congress Cataloging-in-Publication Data

Aleixandre, Vicente, 1898–1984
Shadow of paradise.

Translation of: Sombra del paraíso.
English and Spanish.
I. Harter, Hugh A.   II. Title.
PQ6601.L26S613 1987   861'.62   86-6942
ISBN 0-520-05599-3 (alk. paper)

This publication has been supported by a subvention
from the Program for Cultural Cooperation Between
Spain's Ministry of Culture and North American Universities.

Translator's dedication:
For Frannie

CONTENTS

6

FOREWORD

For Vicente Aleixandre poetry was a daily adventure "toward the ascension of living" ("hacia la ascensión del vivir"). In a letter he wrote to me in February 1959, he explained: "We must not ask of reality that it be transcendent in its every fragment. It is within the rounded entirety of the poem that reality, if treated with minute immediacy, will be transcended, that is, justified." ("No hay que pedir que a cada retazo la realidad quede trascendida: no se trate de eso. Es dentro de su global conjunto del poema donde esa realidad tratada con minuciosa inmediatez quedará trascendida, es decir justificada.")

Shadow of Paradise, perhaps Aleixandre's finest collection, is a radial and radical symphony that conjoins the cosmic and the primal in ways at once harmonious and destructive. In these poems nature's power continually reestablishes itself in human experience; the vigor, violence, and pure vitality of the animal kingdom assume a cognitive awareness that approaches consciousness; and the elemental is ever "the world's only affective reality" ("la única realidad afectiva del mundo"). One thinks of Baudelaire's cats, Blake's tyger, or Rilke's panther. Of the Spanish and Latin American poets, perhaps only García Lorca and Neruda share Aleixandre's understanding of the bestiary.

Clearly, *Shadow of Paradise* is a book about a paradise lost, about the loss of the innocence of love. Paradise and its absence, harmony and destruction, light and shadow, elegy and exaltation: the playing out of human destiny under the immortal canticle of trees, ocean foam, and moonlight: the glittering, unifying energy of erotic forces within a diversity of organic forms.

At the time of his death, Aleixandre was working on a new volume of poetry, *In a Vast Dominion (En un vasto dominio)*. The last poem he sent me was titled "Hair, Fingernail, and Bone" ("El pelo, la uña, y el hueso"). He had chosen to end the poem with the skeleton, the bone inside the flesh:

and deeper within the final
interior weight, the secret mine
of what—only glimpsed—his skeleton . . .
There, terrestrial matter . . .
flesh or smoke, and still deceives
denying the only truth: one day
it shatters, yes, it resuscitates
and pure matter blazes forth.
The truth that is more than human: in it,
the world.

y más adentro el final peso
interior, mina secreta
de lo que—entreverado—, su esqueleto. . . .
Allí la materia terrestre. . .
carne o humo, y aún engaña
negando la verdad única: un día
rompe, sí, resucita
y la materia pura resplandesce.
La verdad más que humana: en ella, el
mundo.

And how close to this truth "that is more than human" the shadow of
paradise becomes for the reader who enters therein, who lives therein,
from childhood to death, as is perhaps our destiny.

Claudio Rodríguez

ACKNOWLEDGMENTS

I completed the basic work on this translation of Aleixandre's *Shadow of Paradise* in Madrid in 1979 under a grant from the Joint Committee for the Cultural and Educational Cooperation between the United States and Spain. I wish to express my thanks to Ramón Bela, Thomas Middleton, and the members of the committee who made that grant possible.

My second debt is to my wife, Frances, who patiently cared for me as I struggled, sometimes night as well as day, with obtuse or resistant passages, while the work sheets piled up precariously. She has been a part of all the revisions and proofing as well and, with the aid of our dear friend Dr. Judith H. Schomber, of Georgia Southern College, gave me invaluable assistance in the preparation of the final manuscript. My mother, Georgiana Harter, has also given insightful suggestions and has sat through many readings of these poems.

I am deeply indebted to the works of several Spanish scholars without whose books and articles neither my translation nor my introduction would have been possible. Carlos Bousoño's work remains a cornerstone in Aleixandre studies. To it we can now add the edition of *Sombra del paraíso* with an excellent introduction by Leopoldo de Luis, the book of José Olivio Jiménez, and the sensitive articles and revelations of José Luis Cano, whose personal reminiscences of his long friendship with Aleixandre have recently appeared in *El País* in Madrid. These eminent scholars have been generous with their time and advice, and I am proud to call them friends.

I am also indebted to the excellent work done by and through the stimulus of Robert Bly and Lewis Hyde in the United States, by Louis M. Bourne in Madrid, and by Lucie Personneaux in France.

Claudio Rodríguez and his lovely wife, Clara Miranda, have been consistently helpful while I worked on the final revisions of the manuscript. Claudio's most perceptive foreword is a deeply appreciated addition to the book.

Other Spanish friends have also been of great help: Amparo Soler of Editorial Castalia; Mercedes Sanjuanbenito, Palmira Pueyo, and María José Lastra of the Instituto Internacional; Luis Felipe de Peñalosa y Contreras, Francisco Otero Martín, and José María Martín Rodríguez of Programas Americanos en Segovia.

In the United States, I have also received much help and encouragement. Drs. Mildred Newcomb and Jeanette Stanton made fine suggestions for revisions. Other friends and colleagues who deserve my special gratitude are: Benjamín and Marianne Balshone, Dana Suesse DeLinks, Amy Einsohn, Robert J. Flanagan, Judith Holzman, Ray Keck III, John Dietrich Mitchell, Ruth Soika, Jacqueline Breslauer Springwater, Ronald Springwater, Douglas W. Steeples, Loretta Tangen, and Madeleine Whiting Wagner.

No acknowledgment would be complete, however, without mention of my dear friend and former professor Stephen Gilman, now Professor Emeritus of Harvard University. It was he who, during a graduate seminar at Ohio State University in the early 1950s, first introduced me to the work of Vicente Aleixandre and to *Shadow of Paradise*. To have worked with Dr. Gilman and with his father-in-law, Jorge Guillén, was one of the great privileges of a lifetime. In a sense, the present volume is a tribute to Gilman and to Guillén, who played a central role in forming my interest in twentieth-century Spanish poetry, and to the memory of Aleixandre himself, who, despite severe illness, wrote to encourage me in my work and gave his approval to this translation.

Hugh A. Harter

INTRODUCTION

When Vicente Aleixandre was named a Nobel laureate in 1977, few North Americans had heard of him. Only two slim volumes of selections from his poetry were available in English translation, both published in limited editions by smaller presses. Since then a generous bilingual edition of selected poems, *A Longing for the Light* (ed. Lewis Hyde; Harper and Row, 1979), has appeared, but the largest portion of the more than eleven hundred pages of poetry and prose that compose Aleixandre's complete works remains inaccessible to English readers.

The present work is the first complete volume of Aleixandre's poems to be published in English translation. In the preface to a volume of his selected poems, Aleixandre remonstrated that to separate a poem from its context, from the body of work to which it belongs, is a kind of mutilation. Thus *Shadow of Paradise* allows English readers for the first time to appreciate the integrity of one of Aleixandre's works in its entirety, as he structured and intended it.

Shadow of Paradise was Aleixandre's fifth volume of poetry to be published, following *Ámbito* (*Ambit*, 1928), *Espadas como labios* (*Swords like Lips*, 1932), *Pasión de la tierra* (*Passion for the Earth*, 1935), and *La destrucción o el amor* (*Destruction or Love*, 1935). For his earliest works, he received Spain's National Prize for Literature in 1933, and *Shadow of Paradise* may be considered both a culmination of those earlier volumes and a harbinger of those that followed. In 1956 Aleixandre explained *Shadow of Paradise*'s pivotal importance in a headnote he wrote for a volume of selected poetry, *Mis mejores poemas (My Best Poems)*:

> This song of the dawn of the world, seen from the vantage point of contemporary man, a canticle of light perceived from the consciousness of the dark (this constant counterpoint, I believe, gives the work its understructure of poignancy), is probably the most widely

known of my books. The first edition was published in 1944. After I had written the first poem, "Springtime on the Earth," I conceived of the work as a whole, and from the initial intuition the book evolved in order and concentrically.

The principal paradisiacal theme is completed, on the one hand, by the vision of the cosmos in its glory, before the appearance of man and, with him, pain and limitation. (These are the seven poems of the series "The Immortals.") Yet to give the book its contrasting dimension and scope, the central nucleus is complemented, on the other hand, by those poems that see man as perishable, conscious of his transience and preoccupied with his end. ("Flesh's Destiny," "To the Sky," "To Man," "Father Mine," "Not Enough," and several more.) This zone anticipates the theme of human life, which received its central development in an earlier work, *History of the Heart*. *Shadow of Paradise* (with *Destruction or Love* and *History of the Heart*) is one of the books of mine that still merits the most esteem.

Aleixandre was born in Seville in 1898. His parents were from well-to-do families, and both the son and his younger sister, Conchita, had a happy childhood. In 1902 the family moved to the city of Málaga, whose sun-drenched Mediterranean seascapes made a profound impression on the young poet: The light that suffuses his adult work is traceable to the dreams and memories of these early years. In 1909 the family moved to Madrid, where Aleixandre would live for the rest of his life. The family was a close one, and even after their mother's death in 1934 and their father's death in 1940, Aleixandre and his sister continued to live in their parents' home.

As a young man, Aleixandre studied and later taught mercantile law at the university. His interest in literature tended toward history and novels of the nineteenth-century realist tradition. Not until the summer of 1917, during a vacation in a mountain village in Ávila, did Aleixandre awaken to poetry. Guided by the young Dámaso Alonso, who was to remain a lifelong friend, Aleixandre began reading the works of Rubén Darío, Gustavo Adolfo Bécquer, and other Spanish and Latin American poets. He soon went on to the works of French, German, and English poets, his facility with languages enabling him to savor these in the original. He began to write poetry, and in 1926 his first poem was published as he was at work on his first volume, *Ámbito* (*Ambit*), which appeared in 1928. By this time, however, Aleixandre had already suffered one of the serious illnesses that were to recur relentlessly throughout his life.

The late 1920s and early 1930s were a heady time for Spanish artists and intellectuals, as the nation entered a second Golden Age in the arts and letters. The cohort of writers known as the Generation of 1898—Miguel de Unamuno, Juan Ramón Jiménez, Antonio Machado, Pío Baroja, Azorín, and Ramón del Valle-Inclán—was at its zenith; a younger group of poets, the Generation of 1927, was coming into its own. This younger generation included Aleixandre, Federico García Lorca, Jorge Guillén, Dámaso Alonso, Rafael Alberti, Luis Cernuda, and Pedro Salinas. During these years, the works of Freud, James Joyce, and the French surrealists were read and discussed; Manuel de Falla was composing orchestral music and ballet suites; Pablo Casals was performing and conducting; Sert, Gris, Miró, and Picasso were exploring the visual arts; and Dalí and Buñuel began producing their controversial surrealistic films.

July 1936 brought a tragic end to this era of brilliant intellectual life in Spain. What at first seemed to be a localized revolt by a group of military officers turned into three years of bloody and devastating civil war. While the immediate causes of the conflict were complex, the confrontation between those Spaniards who favored an absolute monarchy and those favoring a republic had begun a century earlier, when

Napoleon had Ferdinand VII confined and installed his own brother Joseph on the Spanish throne. Throughout the nineteenth century parliamentary government encountered continual opposition, and armed conflict erupted in the 1830s, 1840s, and 1870s. But with the exception of the short-lived republic of 1873–74, the monarchy retained control.

After the forced abdication of Alfonso XIII in 1931, a republic was proclaimed, but there was scant democratic tradition to serve as precedent. In 1936 the Falangist forces, under General Francisco Franco, hoped once and for all to defeat the notion of republican democracy. In this effort Franco received massive military aid, including bombing support, from Nazi Germany and Fascist Italy.

At the war's end, Spain was in ruins: over a million people had been killed, and great numbers wounded; the physical destruction was widespread, and the economy was in a shambles; many survivors were homeless, starving, and impoverished. In effect, two Spains had been created: *España solariega*, the Spain within her boundaries, and *España peregrina*, the thousands of Republicans who sought refuge in France, the Soviet Union, and various countries of the Americas. There has been a tendency, perhaps primarily in the United States, to view *España solariega* as a rather monolithic entity: adherents of General Franco, supporters of Leader, Church, and Fatherland. The truth is far more subtle. Among the Spaniards who remained in their homeland after Franco's victory were people who were neither Fascists nor loyal to Franco's ideology. Some of these Inner Exiles believed in democracy, others in parliamentary monarchy or socialism. Though they could not speak out publicly, they represented the potential for cultural reawakening inside Spain.

Aleixandre was one of the most prominent of these Inner Exiles. During the first two years of the Civil War, tubercular nephritis kept

Aleixandre bedfast. By the war's end, the family home in the Calle Velingtonia had been destroyed by bombardments, and many of Aleixandre's closest friends had died or gone into exile. Lorca had been shot; Unamuno, Valle-Inclán, and Antonio Machado had died; and others had left for the New World. Of Aleixandre's constant companions, only Dámaso Alonso remained. A period of brilliant creativity, a kind of intellectual paradise, had come to an end. During this time of despair, in the aftermath of the Spanish Civil War and at the outbreak of World War II, Aleixandre began to write *Shadow of Paradise*.

In recent years some scholars have criticized *Shadow of Paradise* as imperturbably "classical." They have compared it unfavorably with Dámaso Alonso's *Hijos de la ira (Children of Wrath)*, also published in 1944, with its bitterly incisive social awareness of the suffering and destitution of the period. Others, however, have peered beneath the aestheticism of Aleixandre's lyrics to observe that his basic themes and shadings in *Shadow of Paradise* reflect the profound sense of personal loss, historical tragedy, and national catastrophe that dominated his life and circumstances during the bleak years from 1939 to 1943. For these poems present neither paradise nor a vision of it, but only the illusory, hallucinatory contours of its shadow—diaphanous, intangible, transitory—glimpses of primordial splendor tinged with the nostalgia for worlds that have vanished or perhaps never were, and vague remembrances and intuitions of a remote and intangible utopia, the mythopoetic Málaga of childhood and contemplations of sea, foam, sand, bird, cloud, and stone. The insistent note of loneliness and deprivation acts as a poignant counterpoint to the gorgeous spectacle of nature.

The publication of *Shadow of Paradise* in Madrid in 1944 was an event of singular importance: A major figure of the prewar period whose name and works were officially not to be discussed had been allowed to publish. Although the invasion of Normandy in June 1944 virtually assured Germany's defeat, Fascism was triumphant in Spain. The repression, particularly in the early 1940s, was harsh, with the Gestapo aiding the Spanish police in the cellars of the Dirección General de Seguridad (Internal Security Office) on Madrid's Puerta del Sol.

The fullest portrait of Aleixandre during this period emerges in the recently published reminiscences of the distinguished poet and scholar José Luis Cano. (Cano's memoirs were first made public in 1985 as a series of articles, "Notebooks of Velingtonia," in *El País*, a daily newspaper in Madrid.) Cano had first met Aleixandre in 1929, but the two did not become intimate friends until 1939. In his fascinating chronicle of the preoccupations and fears of Spain's liberal intellectuals during the early years of the Franco regime, Cano describes Aleixandre's prodigious memory, his deep devotion and passionate loyalty to his friends, his readiness to help and to encourage the younger generations who flocked to his home to meet him. In the difficult years of the 1940s and 1950s the house on Calle Velingtonia became a haven and literary mecca. Cano also pictures Aleixandre as a man deeply imbued with democratic principles, a "thundering Jupiter" who spoke out as much as he dared against Fascist totalitarianism, repression, and censorship.

Aleixandre's election in 1949 to the Royal Spanish Academy of Language marked his reemergence as a writer of national prominence. But in 1951 he was threatened with arrest when one of the Fascist hierarchy, "the abominable Vigón" (General Jorge Vigón, Minister of Agriculture), accused him of being a communist, citing "El fusilado," a ballad Aleixandre had written at the outset of the Civil War and published in 1936 in *El mono azul (The Blue Monkey)*, a literary magazine edited by Rafael Alberti. The poem, which tells of the heroism of a Republican soldier who is captured and executed by the Nationalists, seems innocuous today, yet Aleixandre escaped imprisonment only through the efforts of friends in high places. Even his fame and ever-growing prestige were no guarantee of his liberty or safety.

The publication of *Shadow of Paradise* was such an unqualified success that the censors permitted second editions of *Destruction or Love* and *Passion for the Earth*. Thus *Shadow of Paradise* was a turning point in the postwar wasteland, a work that symbolized renewal and reawakening. Consequently, though we may identify the book with a specific time and place in history, we should see it primarily in terms of its aesthetic value. Its themes are the eternal mysteries of man's creation and nature's existence, and their relation to each other: love, desire, solitude, death, and the glories of the scapes of land, sea, and sky. The poet is the lonely exile who perceives glimpses of the Eden man has lost. He is the "timeless prophet" and the seer who "knows how the stone feels." He sees the rain fall, a cloud take shape, a glittering citadel rise phoenixlike above the sea. He discerns messages unrevealed, the tender beauty of the rose, of dawn, night, sunset, and moonscape, and momentarily evokes other hells and other Edens, those of Dante, of Milton, and of the English and German romantics whom he was reading at the time.

In the poems of *Shadow of Paradise*, unlike Aleixandre's earlier works of a surrealistic bent, we do not see the genesis of the world, a universe of primal jungles and destructive fusings that engender life; rather we hear only its echoes. Here a cosmos exists somewhere between dream and waking, between cloud, sky, and reflection, in strange shapes and couplings, in longings that cannot be sated. There is no corporeal Eve to satisfy the poet, although sensuality constantly suffuses the elusive patterns of light and shade, of pastoral settings whose valleys lie within the shadow of death, and whose illusory moments of memory and perception hover on the tentative borders of dream and fantasy. This lost paradise vibrates with ever-intriguing mystery: When and where did this paradise exist? What are its contours? The presence of shadow implies light, and in Aleixandre's work the tenebriousness we associate with Milton's *Paradise Lost* is counterbalanced by luminescences. These poems are shot through with light, and the poet's rejoicing in it. The poet is a modern Prometheus, the seeker of light whose work is a record of a quest and of yearnings that cannot be satisfied.

Aleixandre once described his poetry as a longing or aspiration toward light. In *Shadow of Paradise* we have an abundance of that yearning, closely related to the tone of melancholic solitude that dominates much of the work and reaches a crescendo in "Padre mío" ("Father Mine") and "No basta" ("Not Enough"), two poems of pain, suffering, and bereavement. The first of these two poems is an elegy written in February 1943 for his father, Cirilo, who died on March 9, 1940. The sense of grief and loss that the poem conveys makes this one of the most powerful pieces of the volume. "Father Mine" belongs to a long and rich tradition of Spanish elegiac poetry, whose best-known example is Jorge Manrique's *Coplas por la muerte de su padre (Verses Written on the Death of His Father)*. Manrique, a courtier and soldier in the service of Queen Isabella, expresses his loss in cadenced verses essentially medieval in thought and outlook: the life of this earth is the preparation for that other life beyond death. Manrique experiences both nostalgia and resignation in the face of death's inevitability, but ends his poem on a note of triumph for his father's accomplishments in this life. Aleixandre's poem is marked throughout by despair and desolation and concludes with an expression of the poet's inconsolable and irredeemable solitude.

Two other poems can be identified as autobiographical, "Ciudad del paraíso" ("City of Paradise") and "Cabellera negra" ("Black Tresses"). The former, which has been a favorite of anthologists, is a work of great beauty and also among the most accessible poems in the volume. Aleixandre's later addition of an epigraph dedicating the poem to

Málaga allows the reader to identify the images with a specific place and time, the Málaga of the poet's boyhood, the first years of the century. Memory is soon magically transformed into a shimmering vision halfway between fantasy and myth, and at the poem's end, nostalgia, dream, and vision blend to reinforce the feeling of loss for the Eden of childhood innocence. The second poem, "Black Tresses," rich in sensuality, was inspired by a cabaret performer named Carmen de Granada, for whom, José Luis Cano tells us, Aleixandre felt a passion that absorbed him completely and to whom he wrote his first letters of love, "full of anguish and imaginary jealousies."

The antecedents and affinities of *Shadow of Paradise* are many and complex. Aleixandre knew the *Paradise Lost* of Milton in the original, and he had read the English and German romantics before beginning work on *Shadow of Paradise*. He is one of a long tradition of visionary poets that includes the sixteenth-century Spanish mystics; Gustavo Adolfo Bécquer, Antonio Machado, Juan Ramón Jiménez, and Rubén Darío; Baudelaire and Rimbaud; and the twentieth-century surrealists. His imagery shows an affinity with the Golden Age poets Góngora and Quevedo, and in his poems one hears resonances of the generations of poets who have written of love, of nature, and of solitude. Nevertheless, Aleixandre's work also seems particularly of our century, with its delvings into the inner self and its new interpretation of the universe external to the self.

The translator's responsibility is to transpose as faithfully as possible, but all translations require compromises in fidelity. Beauty and accuracy often involve the translator in a tug-of-war that demands sacrifices of form, cadence, rhythm, rhyme, or content. One also faces the constant problem of interpretation. The translator must comprehend the poet's work, must be a scholar and critic, but must be wary of substituting exposition for transposition. As a scholar, the translator seeks to determine the meaning of a phrase in its original language; as a critic, the translator judges the value of the scholar's work; only then can the translator seek an equivalent phrase in the second language.

Shadow of Paradise presents additional challenges to the translator. Aleixandre has never been considered an easy poet, and though some poems in *Shadow of Paradise* are fairly accessible, many passages allow diverse and even conflicting interpretations. While the collection exhibits a clear thematic unity, there is considerable variety in form, cadence, and subject matter. The longest poem has ninety-three lines, and the two shortest ones, "La palabra" ("Word") and "El aire" ("Air"), only seven. Most, but not all, of the poems are highly irregular in their metrical and strophic forms, with a preponderant number written in unrhymed *versos de arte mayor*, lines of ten or more syllables. Further, Aleixandre's musicality relies on neither assonant nor consonant rhyme; rather, his music is one of interwoven subtle rhythmic patterns, with both traditional and nontraditional meters appearing within the same poem, or even the same line. For an English translator to even suggest these rhythms is quite difficult. English, generally more compact than Spanish, cannot easily and melodically sustain Aleixandre's longest lines. Also, Spanish uses more vowels in proportion to consonants than does English. Consequently, the feel of Spanish hendecasyllables, for example, is approximated in English by tetrameter. In this regard, the eleven poems of *Shadow of Paradise* that are written in heptasyllabic and octosyllabic lines represent unusual challenges.

A final set of tests to the translator's skills is posed by the core vocabulary of *Shadow of Paradise*. Many of the words most often used in this collection are polysyllabic in Spanish but monosyllabic in English: *ave* and *pájaro* = bird; *tierra* = earth; *árbol* = tree; *cielo* = sky; *luna* = moon; *estrella*, *astro*, and *lucero* = star; *piedra* = rock; *hombre* = man; *boca* = mouth; *mano* = hand; *cabellera*, *cabello*, and *pelo* = hair; *corazón*

= heart. For the translator, thus, the task is to avoid producing English verses that are but strings of monosyllables. In addition, the standard English equivalents of certain of Aleixandre's favorite words—*espuma* (the foam of a wave), for example—have, in a sense, been "preempted" by American slang and advertising usage; an Aleixandre seascape should not suggest a travel brochure, nor references to *foam* or *tide* evoke a television ad. The phrase *leve luz*, in which *luz* (light, illumination) is described as *leve* (light in weight), illustrates the problems posed by homographs and homonyms. Obviously, in English one cannot write "the light light"; "tenuous light" seems to me to most clearly and simply express the Spanish original.

The full beauty of Aleixandre's text cannot be captured in translation: *Shadow of Paradise* is not *Sombra del paraíso*. But I hope my effort will serve as a substitute for the reader who knows no Spanish, will help the reader with limited Spanish to approach the original, and perhaps will stimulate some readers to learn Spanish in order to enjoy that language's masterworks. I present this translation in tribute to the man and poet whose death on December 13, 1984, was a loss to his nation, to the Spanish-speaking world, and to the international literary community.

Hugh A. Harter
Madrid, Spain
February 1986

SOMBRA DEL PARAÍSO :: SHADOW OF PARADISE

EL POETA

Para ti, que conoces cómo la piedra canta,
y cuya delicada pupila sabe ya del peso de una montaña sobre un ojo
    dulce,
y cómo el resonante clamor de los bosques se aduerme suave un día en
    nuestras venas;

para ti, poeta, que sentiste en tu aliento
la embestida brutal de las aves celestes,
y en cuyas palabras tan pronto vuelan las poderosas alas de las águilas
como se ve brillar el lomo de los calientes peces sin sonido:
oye este libro que a tus manos envío
con ademán de selva,
pero donde de repente una gota fresquísima de rocío brilla sobre una
    rosa,
o se ve batir el deseo del mundo,
la tristeza que como párpado doloroso
cierra el poniente y oculta el sol como una lágrima oscurecida,
mientras la inmensa frente fatigada
siente un beso sin luz, un beso largo,
unas palabras mudas que habla el mundo finando.

Sí, poeta: el amor y el dolor son tu reino.
Carne mortal la tuya, que, arrebatada por el espíritu,
arde en la noche o se eleva en el mediodía poderoso,
inmensa lengua profética que lamiendo los cielos
ilumina palabras que dan muerte a los hombres.

THE POET

For you, who know how stone sings,
and whose delicate pupil already knows a mountain's weight upon a
    tender eye,
and how the resounding clamor of the forest gently falls asleep one
    day inside our veins;

for you, poet, who in your breath have felt
the brutal onslaught of celestial birds,
and in whose words no sooner take to flight the mighty wings of
    eagles
than one sees the shining backs of silent fiery fish:
hear this book I send into your hands
as if it were a jungle,
but where suddenly a fresh cool drop of dew shines on a rose,
or where the world's desire is seen to throb,
the sadness that like an eyelid weighed with grief
shuts out the west like a darkened tear conceals the sun,
while a weary and colossal brow
feels a lightless kiss, a lengthy kiss,
the voiceless words a dying world articulates.

Yes, poet: love and grief are your kingdom.
Yours is mortal flesh that quickened by the spirit
blazes in the night or rises up at mighty noon,
immense prophetic tongue that licking at the sky
illumines words that bring death to men.

La juventud de tu corazón no es una playa
donde la mar embiste con sus espumas rotas,
dientes de amor que mordiendo los bordes de la tierra,
braman dulce a los seres.

No es ese rayo velador que súbitamente te amenaza,
iluminando un instante tu frente desnuda,
para hundirse en tus ojos e incendiarte, abrasando
los espacios con tu vida que de amor se consume.

No. Esa luz que en el mundo
no es ceniza última,
luz que nunca se abate como polvo en los labios,
eres tú, poeta, cuya mano y no luna
yo vi en los cielos una noche brillando.

Un pecho robusto que reposa atravesado por el mar
respira como la inmensa marea celeste,
y abre sus brazos yacentes y toca, acaricia
los extremos límites de la tierra.

¿Entonces?
Sí, poeta; arroja este libro que pretende encerrar en sus páginas un
    destello del sol,
y mira a la luz cara a cara, apoyada la cabeza en la roca,
mientras tus pies remotísimos sienten el beso postrero del poniente
y tus manos alzadas tocan dulce la luna,
y tu cabellera colgante deja estela en los astros.

The youthfulness of your heart is not a beach
that the sea assails with its shattered foam,
teeth of love, biting at the edges of the earth,
roar sweetly at the creatures there.

It is not the lightning flash that suddenly becomes a threat to you,
lighting up your naked brow an instant,
then to plunge into your eyes inflaming you, burning
vast spaces with your life that is consumed by love.

No. The light that in this world
is not its final ash,
a light that never melts like powder on one's lips,
that light is you, poet, whose hand and not the moon
was what I saw one shining night up in the skies.

A robust breast which lies resting traversed by the sea
breathes like the immense celestial tide
and opens its supine arms and touches, caresses
the farthest limits of the earth.

What then?
Yes, poet; throw aside this book which claims to hold within its
    pages a beam sent from the sun,
and face to face look at the light, your head against the rock,
while your far distant feet feel the setting sun's last kiss
and your hands outstretched gently touch the moon,
and your loose-flowing hair leaves its wake among the stars.

CRIATURAS EN LA AURORA

Vosotros conocisteis la generosa luz de la inocencia.

Entre las flores silvestres recogisteis cada mañana
el último, el pálido eco de la postrer estrella.
Bebisteis ese cristalino fulgor,
que como una mano purísima
dice adiós a los hombres detrás de la fantástica presencia montañosa.
Bajo el azul naciente,
entre las luces nuevas, entre los puros céfiros primeros,
que vencían a fuerza de candor a la noche,
amanecisteis cada día, porque cada día la túnica casi húmeda
se desgarraba virginalmente para amaros,
desnuda, pura, invïolada.

Aparecisteis entre la suavidad de las laderas,
donde la hierba apacible ha recibido eternamente el beso instantáneo
    de la luna.
Ojo dulce, mirada repentina para un mundo estremecido
que se tiende inefable más allá de su misma apariencia.

La música de los ríos, la quietud de las alas,
esas plumas que todavía con el recuerdo del día se plegaron para el
    amor, como para el sueño,
entonaban su quietísimo éxtasis
bajo el mágico soplo de la luz,
luna ferviente que aparecida en el cielo
parece ignorar su efímero destino transparente.

CREATURES IN THE DAWN

You knew the rich full light of innocence.

Each morning from the flowers of the woods you plucked
the last, the pallid echo of a fading star.
You drank the limpid radiance
that like a most pure hand
says farewell to men from beyond the fabled presence of the
    mountains.
Underneath the nascent blue,
among the new stars, among the first pure breezes
that by their very candor vanquished night,
you dawned each day, because each day the barely
moist tunic rended itself like a virgin,
unclad, pure, inviolate, to love you.

Between the sloping hillsides you appeared,
there where the tender grass has felt since time began the moon's
    instantaneous kiss.
Gentle eye, a sudden glance toward a trembling world
that stretches out ineffably beyond its own appearance.

The melody of rivers, the quietness of wings,
those feathers that, still remembering the day, folded back for love,
    as though for sleep,
intoned their wholly silent ecstasy
beneath the magic gust of light,
the fervent moon that once it has appeared up in the sky
seems to ignore its ephemeral transparent destiny.

La melancólica inclinación de los montes
no significaba el arrepentimiento terreno
ante la inevitable mutación de las horas:
era más bien la tersura, la mórbida superficie del mundo
que ofrecía su curva como un seno hechizado.

Allí vivisteis. Allí cada día presenciasteis la tierra,
la luz, el calor, el sondear lentísimo
de los rayos celestes que adivinaban las formas,
que palpaban tiernamente las laderas, los valles,
los ríos con su ya casi brillante espada solar,
acero vívido que guarda aún, sin lágrima, la amarillez tan íntima,
la plateada faz de la luna retenida en sus ondas.

Allí nacían cada mañana los pájaros,
sorprendentes, novísimos, vividores, celestes.
Las lenguas de la inocencia
no decían palabras:
entre las ramas de los altos álamos blancos
sonaban casi también vegetales, como el soplo en las frondas.
¡Pájaros de la dicha inicial, que se abrían
estrenando sus alas, sin perder la gota virginal del rocío!

Las flores salpicadas, las apenas brillantes florecillas del soto,
eran blandas, sin grito, a vuestras plantas desnudas.
Yo os vi, os presentí cuando el perfume invisible
besaba vuestros pies, insensibles al beso.

The mountain's melancholy inclination
did not signify sorrow of an earthly kind
confronted with the hours' inevitable mutation:
it was more like the smoothness, the morbid surface of the world
that exposed its arching curve like a breast bewitched.

There you lived. There every day you were witness to the earth,
the light, the warmth, the slow and solemn probings
of celestial rays that anticipated forms,
that tenderly caressed the slopes, the valleys,
the rivers with their lightly gleaming solar sword,
vivid steel that still retains, without a tear, the yellow glow so
    intimate,
the silvered image of the moon held captive in its waves.

There every dawn the birds were born,
astonishing, freshly new, full of life, celestial.
The tongues of innocence
said no word:
among the branches of tall white poplar trees
they too made sounds almost like plants, like a gust of wind among
    the leaves.
Birds of primeval happiness that stretched
to try their wings without losing the virginal drop of dew!

Flowers besprinkled, the barely brilliant blossoms of the copse,
were tamed, silenced, at your feet unclothed.
I saw you, felt your presence when the unseen fragrance
kissed your feet, unfeeling to that kiss.

¡No crueles: dichosos! En las cabezas desnudas
brillaban acaso las hojas iluminadas del alba.
Vuestra frente se hería, ella misma, contra los rayos dorados,
    recientes, de la vida,
del sol, del amor, del silencio bellísimo.

No había lluvia, pero unos dulces brazos
parecían presidir a los aires,
y vuestros cuellos sentían su hechicera presencia,
mientras decíais palabras a las que el sol naciente daba magia de
    plumas.

No, no es ahora cuando la noche va cayendo,
también con la misma dulzura pero con un levísimo vapor de ceniza,
cuando yo correré tras vuestras sombras amadas.
Lejos están las inmarchitas horas matinales,
imagen feliz de la aurora impaciente,
tierno nacimiento de la dicha en los labios,
en los seres vivísimos que yo amé en vuestras márgenes.

El placer no tomaba el temeroso nombre de placer,
ni el turbio espesor de los bosques hendidos,
sino la embriagadora nitidez de las cañadas abiertas
donde la luz se desliza con sencillez de pájaro.

Por eso os amo, inocentes, amorosos seres mortales
de un mundo virginal que diariamente se repetía
cuando la vida sonaba en las gargantas felices
de las aves, los ríos, los aires y los hombres.

Not in cruelty: in happiness! On uncovered heads
shined down perhaps the luminescent leaves of dawn.
Your very brow struck hard against the gilded, newborn rays of life,
of sun, of love, of resplendent silence.

There was no rain, but gentle arms
seemed to dominate the air,
and your shoulders felt their enchanting presence,
while you addressed those beings that the dawning sun adorned with
    feathered magic.

No, it is not now while night is falling,
still with the same sweetness but with a weightless mist of ash,
that I shall run pursuing those beloved shadows.
Far distant are the pristine hours of the morning,
the happy image of impatient dawn,
the tender birth of happiness on your lips,
on the life-filled beings that I loved within your boundaries.

Pleasure did not take the fearful name of pleasure
nor the turbid density of forests cleft in two,
but the intoxicating clarity of open gullies
where light flows in with the litheness of a bird.

That is why I love you, innocent and loving mortal beings
from a virgin world that daily did repeat itself,
when life resounded deeply in the happy throats
of birds, or rivers, air and men.

DESTINO TRÁGICO

Confundes ese mar silencioso que adoro
con la espuma instantánea del viento entre los árboles.

Pero el mar es distinto.
No es viento, no es su imagen.
No es el resplandor de un beso pasajero,
ni es siquiera el gemido de unas alas brillantes.

No confundáis sus plumas, sus alisadas plumas,
con el torso de una paloma.
No penséis en el pujante acero del águila.
Por el cielo las garras poderosas detienen el sol.
Las águilas oprimen a la noche que nace,
la estrujan —todo un río de último resplandor va a los mares—
y la arrojan remota, despedida, apagada,
allí donde el sol de mañana duerme niño sin vida.

Pero el mar, no. No es piedra
esa esmeralda que todos amasteis en las tardes sedientas.
No es piedra rutilante toda labios tendiéndose,
aunque el calor tropical haga a la playa latir,
sintiendo el rumoroso corazón que la invade.

Muchas veces pensasteis en el bosque.
Duros mástiles altos,

TRAGIC DESTINY

You confuse this silent sea that I adore
with the wind's instantaneous spray among the trees.

But the sea is something else.
It is not wind, is not its image.
Nor is it splendor from a passing kiss,
not even the lamentation of several gleaming wings.

Do not confuse its feathers, its burnished feathers,
with the torso of a dove.
Do not think about the eagle's forceful steel.
In the sky its sinewed claws hold back the sun.
The eagles crush the night that is born,
they drain it dry—a whole river of final splendor flows down to the
    seas—
and cast it there, remote, abandoned and devoid of light,
there where tomorrow's sun sleeps like a lifeless child.

But the sea, no. It is not stone,
that emerald you all so loved on thirsty afternoons.
It is not stone that sparkling purses out like lips,
although the torrid heat makes the shoreline palpitate,
as it feels the murmuring heart that is invading it.

Frequently you thought about the woods.
Hard, tall masts,

árboles infinitos
bajo las ondas adivinasteis poblados de unos pájaros de espumosa
    blancura.
Visteis los vientos verdes
inspirados moverlos,
y escuchasteis los trinos de unas gargantas dulces:
ruiseñor de los mares, noche tenue sin luna,
fulgor bajo las ondas donde pechos heridos
cantan tibios en ramos de coral con perfume.

Ah, sí, yo sé lo que adorasteis.
Vosotros pensativos en la orilla,
con vuestra mejilla en la mano aún mojada,
mirasteis esas ondas, mientras acaso pensabais en un cuerpo:
un solo cuerpo dulce de un animal tranquilo.
Tendisteis vuestra mano y aplicasteis su calor
a la tibia tersura de una piel aplacada.
¡Oh suave tigre a vuestros pies dormido!

Sus dientes blancos visibles en las fauces doradas,
brillaban ahora en paz. Sus ojos amarillos,
minúsculas guijas casi de nácar al poniente,
cerrados, eran todo silencio ya marino.
Y el cuerpo derramado, veteado sabiamente de una onda poderosa,
era bulto entregado, caliente, dulce sólo.

infinity of trees
beneath the swelling waves you conjectured the dwellings of birds of
    whitest foam.
You saw the green winds
full of breath move them,
and you listened to the trillings of their tender throats:
nightingale of the seas, insubstantial moonless night,
a glow beneath the waves where wounded breasts
sing warmly on the coral's perfumed boughs.

Ah yes, I know what you adored.
You sat thinking by the shore,
your cheek at rest upon your still-moist hand,
you watched those waves and thought perhaps about a body:
a single tender body of a tranquil animal.
You stretched your hand out and you gave your warmth
to the tepid smoothness of its quiescent skin.
Oh docile tiger sleeping at your feet!

His teeth of white visible in his golden jaws
now were gleaming peacefully. His yellow eyes,
small nacrous pebbles in the setting sun,
tight-closed, were already all silence of the sea.
And the body that poured forth, expertly striped by a mighty wave,
was a submissive, warm, and fully gentle shape.

Pero de pronto os levantasteis.
Habíais sentido las alas oscuras,
envío mágico del fondo que llama a los corazones.
Mirasteis fijamente el empezado rumor de los abismos.
¿Qué formas contemplasteis? ¿Qué signos inviolados,
qué precisas palabras que la espuma decía,
dulce saliva de unos labios secretos
que se entreabren, invocan, someten, arrebatan?
El mensaje decía . . .

Yo os vi agitar los brazos. Un viento huracanado
movió vuestros vestidos iluminados por el poniente trágico.
Vi vuestra cabellera alzarse traspasada de luces,
y desde lo alto de una roca instantánea
presencié vuestro cuerpo hendir los aires
y caer espumante en los senos del agua;
vi dos brazos largos surtir de la negra presencia
y vi vuestra blancura, oí el último grito,
cubierto rápidamente por los trinos alegres de los ruiseñores del
    fondo.

But soon thereafter you arose.
You had felt the somber wings,
the magic message from the depths that calls to hearts.
You contemplated steadily the incipient murmur from the abyss.
What figures did you gaze at? What signs, inviolate,
what specific words the foam was saying,
the sweet saliva of those secret lips
that barely open, call, subdue, and move to ecstasy?
The message said . . .

I saw you wave your arms. A hurricane wind
moved your garments illumined by the sunset's tragic glow.
I saw your tresses rise up suffused with light,
and one brief instant from high upon a rock
I bore witness as your body cleft the air
and fell sparkling on the water's breasts;
I saw two long arms stretching from the black presence
and I saw your whiteness, I heard your final cry,
quickly muffled by the happy trills of nightingales in the
    background.

SIERPE DE AMOR

Pero ¿a quién amas, dime?
Tendida en la espesura,
entre los pájaros silvestres, entre las frondas vivas,
rameado tu cuerpo de luces deslumbrantes,
dime a quién amas, indiferente, hermosa,
bañada en vientos amarillos del día.

Si a tu lado deslizo
mi oscura sombra larga que te desea;
si sobre las hojas en que reposas yo me arrastro, crujiendo
levemente tentador y te espío,
no amenazan tu oído mis sibilantes voces,
porque perdí el hechizo que mis besos tuvieran.

El lóbulo rosado donde con diente pérfido
mi marfil incrustara tropical en tu siesta,
no mataría nunca, aunque diera mi vida
al morder dulcemente sólo un sueño de carne.

Unas palabras blandas de amor, no mi saliva,
no mi verde veneno de la selva, en tu oído
vertería, desnuda imagen, diosa que regalas tu cuerpo
a la luz, a la gloria fulgurante del bosque.

Entre tus pechos vivos levemente mi forma
deslizaría su beso sin fin, como una lengua,
cuerpo mío infinito de amor que día a día
mi vida entera en tu piel consumara.

SERPENT OF LOVE

But tell me, whom do you love?
Stretched out in the undergrowth,
among the sylvan birds, among the living fronds,
your body patterned by a daze of light,
tell me whom you love, indifferent, beautiful,
bathed in yellow winds of day.

If at your side I slip
my long dark shadow which yearns for you;
if on the leaves where you rest I crawl, with rustling sound,
a gentle tempter, and spy on you,
the hissing of my voice should be no threat to you,
for I have lost the sorcery my lips once held.

The rosy lobe on which a perfidious tooth,
my ivory fang, might torridly invade your sleep,
would never kill, although I'd give my life itself
if I could softly bite so much as a dream of flesh.

Some soft words of love, not my saliva,
nor my green jungle's venom, would I pour
into your ear, naked image, goddess who offers her body
to the light and to the lustrous glory of the woods.

Between your living breasts my form would gently
slip its endless kiss, like a tongue,
my body limitless with love that day by day
would consume my entire life within your skin.

Erguido levemente sobre tu seno mismo,
mecido, ebrio en la música secreta de tu aliento,
yo miraría tu boca luciente en la espesura,
tu mejilla solar que vida ofrece
y el secreto tan leve de tu pupila oculta
en la luz, en la sombra, en tu párpado intacto.

Yo no sé qué amenaza de lumbre hay en la frente,
cruje en tu cabellera rompiente de resoles,
y vibra y aun restalla en los aires, como un eco
de ti toda hermosísima, halo de luz que mata.

Si pico aquí, si hiendo mi deseo, si en tus labios
penetro, una gota caliente
brotará en su tersura, y mi sangre agolpada en mi boca,
querrá beber, brillar de rubí duro,
bañada en ti, sangre hermosísima, sangre de flor turgente,
fuego que me consume centelleante y me aplaca
la dura sed de tus brillos gloriosos.

Boca con boca dudo si la vida es el aire
o es la sangre. Boca con boca muero,
respirando tu llama que me destruye.
Boca con boca siento que hecho luz me desahogo,
hecho lumbre que en el aire fulgura.

Erect above your breast and swaying to and fro,
intoxicated with the secret music of your breath,
I would watch your shining mouth in the undergrowth,
your sunlit cheek that proffers life,
and the trifling secret of your pupil hidden
in the light, in the shadows, in your untouched eyelid.

I do not know what threat of fire there is upon your brow,
that crackles in your hair shot through with sun's reflections,
that quivers and even crackles in the air like an echo
of you in your perfect beauty, a halo of light that kills.

If I bite here, if I split through desire, if through your
lips I penetrate, a fevered drop
will burst into its smooth confines, and my blood that floods my
    mouth,
will want to drink, to shine like hard ruby,
bathed in you, exquisite blood, swollen flower's blood,
fire that burns me in its dazzle and that soothes
my driving thirst for your resplendent glories.

Mouth against mouth, I wonder if life is air
or blood. Mouth against mouth I die,
inhaling your flame that destroys me.
Mouth against mouth I find release, transformed into light,
transformed into flame that flashes in the air.

EL RÍO

Tú eres, ligero río,
el que miro de lejos, en ese continente que rompió con la tierra.
Desde esta inmensa llanura donde el cielo aboveda
a la frente y cerrado brilla puro, sin amor, yo diviso
aquel cielo ligero, viajador, que bogaba
sobre ti, río tranquilo que arrojabas hermosas
a las nubes en el mar, desde un seno encendido.

Desde esta lisa tierra esteparia veo la curva
de los dulces naranjos. Allí libre la palma,
el albérchigo, allí la vid madura,
allí el limonero que sorbe al sol su jugo agraz en la mañana virgen;
allí el árbol celoso que al humano rehúsa su flor, carne sólo,
magnolio dulce, que te delatas siempre por el sentido que de ti se
     enajena.

Allí el río corría, no azul, no verde o rosa, no amarillo, río ebrio,
río que matinal atravesaste mi ciudad inocente,
ciñéndola con una guirnalda temprana, para acabar desciñéndola,
dejándola desnuda y tan confusa al borde de la verde montaña,
donde siempre virginal ahora fulge, inmarchita en el eterno día.

Tú, río hermoso que luego, más liviano que nunca, entre bosques
     felices

THE RIVER

It is you, weightless river,
that I see afar, on the continent that broke away from earth.
From this boundless plain where the sky arches
a vaulted brow and darkly shines pure and without love,
I behold that weightless sky, a voyager sailing
above you, tranquil river that hurls the clouds
in all their beauty from your fiery breast into the sea.

From this flat plain, I see the curving form
of sweet orange trees. There the tropic palm is born,
the clingstone peach, there the vine ripens,
there the lemon tree that imbibes its bitter juice in the virgin
    morning's sun;
there the tree that zealously denies to men its flower, flesh only,
sweet magnolia, you who always betray yourself by the intoxicating
    fragrance that emanates from you.

There the river flowed, not blue, not green or rose, not yellow, a
    drunken river,
the river that crossed my innocent city every morning,
engirdling her with early garlands, then undoing them,
leaving her naked and confused beside the verdant mountain,
where still virginal she shines now, untainted in the eternal day.

You, comely river that afterwards, more faithless than before
    between the happy woodlands

corrías hacia valles no pisados por la planta del hombre.
Río que nunca fuiste suma de tristes lágrimas,
sino acaso rocío milagroso que una mano reúne.
Yo te veo gozoso todavía allá en la tierra que nunca fue del todo
    separada de estos límites en que habito.

Mira a los hombres, perseguidos no por tus aves,
no por el cántico de que el humano olvidóse por siempre.
Escuchándoos estoy, pájaros imperiosos,
que exigís al desnudo una planta ligera,
desde vuestras reales ramas estremecidas,
mientras el sol melodioso templa dulce las ondas
como rubias espaldas, de ese río extasiado.

Ligeros árboles, maravillosos céspedes silenciosos,
blandos lechos tremendos en el país sin noche,
crespusculares velos que dulcemente afligidos
desde el poniente envían un adiós sin tristeza.

Oyendo estoy a la espuma como garganta quejarse.
Volved, sonad, guijas que al agua en lira convertís.
Cantad eternamente sin nunca hallar el mar.
Y oigan los hombres con menguada tristeza
el son divino. ¡Oh río que como luz hoy veo,
que como brazo hoy veo de amor que a mí me llama!

flowed toward valleys where no foot of man had ever stepped.
River that never was the confluence of sad tears,
but perhaps a miraculous dew a hand conjoins.
I see you there still joyous on the earth that was never fully sundered
    from those outposts where I live.

Look at mankind, pursued not by your birds,
nor even by the canticle that men have forgotten for all time.
I am listening to your song, imperious birds,
as from your regal trembling boughs
you demand of the nude that he be fleet of foot,
as the sun's soft melody of light moderates the waves
like golden shoulders of that enraptured river.

Weightless trees, marvelous silent lawns of grass,
smooth tremendous couches in a nightless land,
the gently grieving veils of twilight
send from the setting sun a farewell devoid of sadness.

I am listening to the foam that like a throat complains.
Come back, ring out, pebbles that transformed the water into lyre.
Sing endlessly and never find the sea.
And may men with lessened sadness hear
the lovely sound. Oh river that today I see as light,
that today I see like an arm of love calling out to me!

NACIMIENTO DEL AMOR

¿Cómo nació el amor? Fue ya en otoño.
Maduro el mundo,
no te aguardaba ya. Llegaste alegre,
ligeramente rubia, resbalando en lo blando
del tiempo. Y te miréo. ¡Qué hermosa
me pareciste aún, sonriente, vívida,
frente a la luna aún niña, prematura en la tarde,
sin luz, graciosa en aires dorados; como tú,
que llegabas sobre el azul, sin beso,
pero con dientes claros, con impaciente amor.

Te miré. La tristeza
se encogía a lo lejos, llena de paños largos,
como un poniente graso que sus ondas retira.
Casi una lluvia fina —¡el cielo, azul!— mojaba
tu frente nueva. ¡Amante, amante era el destino
de la luz! Tan dorada te miré que los soles
apenas se atrevían a insistir, a encenderse
por ti, de ti, a darte siempre
su pasión luminosa, ronda tierna
de soles que giraban en torno a ti, astro dulce,
en torno a un cuerpo casi transparente, gozoso,
que empapa luces húmedas, finales, de la tarde,
y vierte, todavía matinal, sus auroras.

THE BIRTH OF LOVE

How was love born? It came about in autumn.
The world in middle age
did not expect you any more. You arrived a happy babe,
somewhat fair-complexioned, slipping into the softness
of time. And I looked at you. How lovely still
you seemed to me, smiling, vivid,
facing toward the still infant moon, in the evening premature,
without light, a dainty child in golden air; like you
who came across the azure sky, without a kiss,
but with bright teeth, with impatient love.

I looked at you. Sadness
was crouching in the distance, swathed in flowing robes
like a thick setting sun that draws back its waves.
An almost misty rain—the sky so blue!—bedewed
your newborn brow. Light's destiny was love,
to be a lover! So golden did I see you there that the suns
hardly dared persist, or burst in flame
for you, from you, to give to you forever
their luminescent passion, the tender round
of suns that turned around you, gentle star,
around a body half-transparent, full of joy,
that absorbs the humid, final lights of close of day
and sheds, still matinal, its auroral hues.

Eras tú amor, destino, final amor luciente,
nacimiento penúltimo hacia la muerte acaso.
Pero no. Tú asomaste. ¿Eras ave, eras cuerpo,
alma sólo? ¡Ah, tu carne traslúcida
besaba como dos alas tibias,
como el aire que mueve un pecho respirando,
y sentí tus palabras, tu perfume,
y en el alma profunda, clarividente
diste fondo! Calado de ti hasta el tuétano de la luz,
sentí tristeza, tristeza del amor: amor es triste.
En mi alma nacía el día. Brillando
estaba de ti; tu alma en mí estaba.
Sentí dentro, en mi boca, el sabor a la aurora.
Mis sentidos dieron su dorada verdad. Sentí a los pájaros
en mi frente piar, ensordeciendo
mi corazón. Miré por dentro
los ramos, las cañadas luminosas, las alas variantes,
y un vuelo de plumajes de color, de encendidos
presentes me embriagó, mientras todo mi ser a un mediodía,
raudo, loco, creciente se encendiaba
y mi sangre ruidosa se despeñaba en gozos
de amor, de luz, de plenitud, de espuma.

It was you love, destiny, a final shining love,
penultimate birth perhaps near death.
But no. You did appear. Were you bird, were you body,
only soul? Ah, your translucid flesh
gave kisses like a pair of tepid wings,
like air that fills a breathing breast,
and I felt your words, your perfume,
and in my deepest soul, with sure perception
you cast anchor. Soaked to the very marrow with the light of you,
I felt sadness, love's sadness: love is sad.
In my soul day was dawning. I was aglow
with you; your soul was in me.
I felt inside, inside my mouth, the flavor of the dawn.
My senses registered its golden truth. I heard the birds
chirping above my head and making my heart
go deaf. I saw inside myself
the boughs, the luminescent valleys, the changing wings,
and a flight of feathers brilliant-hued and of fiery
presents made me drunk, while all my being like a noonday sun,
impetuous, insensate, rising up burst into flame,
and my blood noisily hurled itself into the joys
of love, of light, of plenitude, of foam.

ARCÁNGEL DE LAS TINIEBLAS

Me miras con tus ojos azules,
nacido del abismo.
Me miras bajo tu crespa cabellera nocturna,
helado cielo fulgurante que adoro.
Bajo tu frente nívea
dos arcos duros amenazan mi vida.
No me fulmines, cede, oh, cede amante y canta.
Naciste de un abismo entreabierto
en el nocturno insomnio de mi pavor solitario.
Humo abisal cuajante te formó, te precisó hermosísimo.
Adelantaste tu planta, todavía brillante de la roca pelada,
y subterráneamente me convocaste al mundo,
al infierno celeste, oh arcángel de la tiniebla.

Tu cuerpo resonaba remotamente allí, en el horizonte,
humoso mar espeso de deslumbrantes bordes,
labios de muerte bajo nocturnas aves
que graznaban deseo con pegajosas plumas.

Tu frente altiva rozaba estrellas
que afligidamente se apagaban sin vida,
y en la altura metálica, lisa, dura, tus ojos
eran las luminarias de un cielo condenado.

Respirabas sin vientos, pero en mi pecho daba
aletazos sombríos un latido conjunto.
Oh, no, no me toquéis, brisas frías,
labios larguísimos, membranosos avances
de un amor, de una sombra, de una muerte besada.

ARCHANGEL OF THE SHADOWS

You look at me with your dark blue eyes,
born from the abyss.
You look at me from underneath your curly night-black hair,
the frosty shining sky that I adore.
Beneath your snowy forehead
two harsh arches threaten my life.
Do not strike me down, yield, oh yield lovingly and sing.
You were born from a yawning chasm in the night's insomnia of my
    solitary fear.
A congealing vapor from the depths gave form to you, defined you
    in greatest beauty.
You stretched out your foot, still gleaming from the naked rock,
and from dark abysses in the earth you summoned me into the
    world,
to hell's celestial realms, oh archangel of the shadows.

Your body pulsed remotely there, on the horizon,
a thick and misty sea of dazzling shores,
lips of death beneath nocturnal birds
that with viscous feathers cawed desire.

Your haughty brow grazed the stars
that grievingly grew dim with lifelessness,
and in that metallic height, smooth and hard, your eyes
were like two lanterns in a sky condemned.

You were drawing windless breath, but in my breast
a kindred throbbing caused dark wingbeats.
No, do not touch me, chilling breezes,
outstretched lips, membranous advances
of a love, of a shadow, of a death that has been kissed.

A la mañana siguiente algo amanecía
apenas entrevisto tras el monte azul, leve,
quizá ilusión, aurora, ¡oh matinal deseo!,
quizá destino cándido bajo la luz del día.

Pero la noche al cabo cayó pesadamente.
Oh labios turbios, oh carbunclo encendido,
oh torso que te erguiste, tachonado de fuego,
duro cuerpo de lumbre tenebrosa, pujante,
que incrustaste tu testa en los cielos helados.

Por eso yo te miro. Porque la noche reina.
Desnudo ángel de luz muerta, dueño mío.
Por eso miro tu frente, donde dos arcos impasibles
gobiernan mi vida sobre un mundo apagado.

The morning after that one, something barely visible
beyond the mist-blue mountain's peak appeared,
perhaps illusion, dawn, oh morning's fresh desire!
perhaps bright destiny beneath the light of day.

But night at last with heavy darkness fell.
Oh turbid lips, oh inflamed garnet,
oh torso that rose up spangled with flame,
hard body of penumbral mighty gleam
that etched your head upon the frozen sky.

Because of that I gaze at you. Because the night prevails.
Nude angel of the light that died, master mine.
Because of that I look upon your brow where two impassive arches
govern my life upon a lightless world.

PODERÍO DE LA NOCHE

El sol cansado de vibrar en los cielos
resbala lentamente en los bordes de la tierra,
mientras su gran ala fugitiva
se arrastra todavía con el delirio de la luz,
iluminando la vacía prematura tristeza.

Labios volantes, aves que suplican al día
su perduración frente a la vasta noche amenazante,
surcan un cielo que pálidamente se irisa
borrándose ligero hacia lo oscuro.

Un mar, pareja de aquella larguísima ala de la luz,
bate su color azulado
abiertamente, cálidamente aún,
con todas sus vivas plumas extendidas.

¿Qué coyuntura, qué vena, qué plumón estirado
como un pecho tendido a la postrera caricia del sol
alza sus espumas besadas,
su amontonado corazón espumoso,
sus ondas levantadas
que invadirán la tierra en una última búsqueda de la luz escapándose?

Yo sé cuán vasta soledad en las playas,
qué vacía presencia de un cielo aún no estrellado,
vela cóncavamente sobre el titánico esfuerzo,
sobre la estéril lucha de la espuma y la sombra.

El lejano horizonte, tan infinitamente solo
como un hombre en la muerte,
envía su vacío, resonancia de un cielo
donde la luna anuncia su nada ensordecida.

Un claror lívido invade un mundo donde nadie
alza su voz gimiente,
donde los peces huidos a los profundos senos misteriosos
apagan sus ojos lucientes de fósforo,
y donde los verdes aplacados,
los silenciosos azules
suprimen sus espumas enlutadas de noche.

¿Qué inmenso pájaro nocturno,
qué silenciosa pluma total y neutra
enciende fantasmas de luceros en su piel sibilina,
piel única sobre la cabeza de un hombre
que en una roca duerme su estrellado transcurso?

El rumor de la vida
sobre el gran mar oculto
no es el viento, aplacado,
no es el rumor de una brisa ligera que en otros días felices
rizara los luceros,
acariciando las pestañas amables,
los dulces besos que mis labios os dieron,
oh estrellas en la noche,
estrellas fijas enlazadas
por mis vivos deseos.

POWER OF THE NIGHT

The sun grown tired of throbbing in the sky
glides slowly on the edges of the earth,
while its great wing, a fugitive,
still flutters with the delirium of the light,
illuminating the empty premature sadness.

Lips in flight, birds that beg of day
that it endure despite the menace of vast night,
stream across the sky that pallidly grows iridescent
as it slowly fades into the dark.

A sea, twin of that great long wing of light,
flaps its bluish color
in a frank appeal, still holding warmth,
with all its vivid plumage stretched full-length.

What body's joint, what vein, what downy feathers spread
like a bosom reaching for the dying sun's caress
lifts up its kissed foam,
its massive foamy heart,
its surging waves
that will invade the earth in one last search for the fleeting light?

I know how vast a solitude upon the shore,
what an empty presence of a sky now devoid of stars,
maintains a hollow vigil over that titanic effort,
over the sterile conflict of the foam and shadow.

The distant horizon, as infinitely lonely
as a man in his death,
sends forth its void, the resonance of a sky
in which the moon proclaims its muted nothingness.

A livid gleam invades a world where no one
lifts his voice in grief,
where fish that fled to the deep mysterious breasts
have closed their shining phosphorescent eyes,
and where now tranquil greens
and silent blues
suppress the foam that night has draped with black.

What immense nocturnal bird,
what total silent and neutral feather
lights the ghostly lanterns in its enigmatic flesh,
sole flesh above the head of man
who lying on a rock dreams his star-filled course?

The muffled sound of life
across the vast mysterious sea
is neither wind now quieted
nor the murmur of a gentle breeze that on other happy days
would ripple through the starry host
and caress the lovely lashes,
the sweet kisses that my lips gave you,
oh stars of night,
fixed stars entwined
by my intense desires.

Entonces la juventud, la ilusión, el amor encantado
rizaban un cabello gentil que el azul confundía
diariamente con el resplandor estrellado del sol sobre la arena.
Emergido de la espuma con la candidez de la Creación reciente,
mi planta imprimía su huella en las playas
con la misma rapidez de las barcas,
ligeros envíos de un mar benévolo bajo el gran brazo del aire,
continuamente aplacado por una mano dichosa acariciando sus
    espumas vivientes.

Pero lejos están los remotos días
en que el amor se confundía con la pujanza de la naturaleza radiante
y en que un mediodía feliz y poderoso
henchía un pecho, con un mundo a sus plantas.

Esta noche, cóncava y desligada,
no existe más que como existen las horas,
como el tiempo, que pliega
lentamente sus silenciosas capas de ceniza,
borrando la dicha de los ojos, los pechos y las manos,
y hasta aquel silencioso calor
que dejara en los labios el rumor de los besos.

Por eso yo no veo, como no mira nadie,
esa presente bóveda nocturna,
vacío reparador de la muerte no esquiva,

In those days youth, illusion, love's enchantment
rumpled up my tousled hair, which ocean's blue would
daily mingle with the sun's starry splendor on the sand.
Emerging from the foamy surf with the innocence of Creation newly
    born,
my foot would press its imprint on the shore,
with the same swiftness of the ships,
rapid messages from a sea benevolent beneath the air's great arm,
continuously soothed by a favored hand that caresses its living foams.

But distant are those far-off days
when love would blend with all the might of nature in its radiance
and when a happy and forceful noonday sun
filled up a breast, with a world lying at its feet.

This night, concave and disentangled,
has no more existence than the hours have,
or than time, that slowly
spreads its silent cloaks of ashes,
blotting out the joy of eyes, of breasts and hands,
and even that silent warmth
that left on the lips the murmur of its kisses.

And so I do not see, as no one sees,
that present dome of night,
that void restorer of never-timid death,

inmensa, invasora realidad intangible
que ha deslizado cautelosa
su hermético oleaje de plomo ajustadísimo.

Otro mar muerto, bello,
abajo acaba de asfixiarse. Unos labios
inmensos cesaron de latir, y en sus bordes
aún se ve deshacerse un aliento, una espuma.

immense intangible reality
that has cunningly imposed
its hermetic surge of tightly fitted lead.

Another lifeless sea, a lovely one
that lies below, has been asphyxiated. Vast lips
have ceased to throb, and on their edges
one still can see a breath, a foam dissolve.

2

DIOSA

Dormida sobre el tigre,
su leve trenza yace.
Mirad su bulto. Alienta
sobre la piel hermosa,
tranquila, soberana.
¿Quién puede osar, quién sólo
sus labios hoy pondría
sobre la luz dichosa
que, humana apenas, sueña?
Miradla allí. ¡Cuán sola!
¡Cuán intacta! ¿Tangible?
Casi divina, leve
el seno se alza, cesa,
se yergue, abate; gime
como el amor. Y un tigre
soberbio la sostiene
como la mar hircana,
donde flotase extensa,
feliz, nunca ofrecida.

¡Ah, mortales! No, nunca;
desnuda, nunca vuestra.
Sobre la piel hoy ígnea
miradla, exenta: es diosa.

THE GODDESS

As she sleeps upon the tiger,
her pale tresses lie at rest.
Behold her ample form. Upon
that lovely skin she breathes,
sovereign in calm serenity.
Who would even dare, who try
today to place his lips
upon that radiant light
that, almost human, dreams?
Behold her there. How much alone!
How untouched! But touchable?
Almost divine, as light as air,
her breast in sleep expands and falls,
then swells and drops again; she
moans with love's sound. And, superb,
a tiger forms for her a couch,
a striped and furrowed sea
on which to float full-stretched,
in happy ease, never to be touched.

No, mortals! No, not ever;
though naked, she is never yours.
Against her skin now igneous,
behold her there: a goddess.

LA VERDAD

¿Qué sonríe en la sombra sin muros que ensordece
mi corazón? ¿Qué soledad levanta
sus torturados brazos sin luna y grita herida
a la noche? ¿Quién canta sordamente en las ramas?

Pájaros no: memoria de pájaros. Sois eco,
sólo eco, pluma vil, turbia escoria, muerta materia sorda
aquí en mis manos. Besar una ceniza
no es besar el amor. Morder una seca rama
no es poner estos labios brillantes sobre un seno
cuya turgencia tibia dé lumbre a estos marfiles
rutilantes. ¡El sol, el sol deslumbra!

Separar un vestido crujiente, resto inútil
de una ciudad. Poner desnudo
el manantial, el cuerpo luminoso, fluyente,
donde sentir la vida ferviente entre los ramos
tropicales, quemantes, que un ecuador empuja.

Bebed, bebed la rota pasión de un mediodía
que en el cenit revienta sus luces y os abrasa
volcadamente entero, y os funde. ¡Muerte hermosa vital,
ascua del día! ¡Selva virgen que en llamas te destruyes!

TRUTH

What smiles in the wall-less shadow that deafens
my heart? What solitude raises
its tortured, moonless arms and, wounded, cries
into the night? Who sings in muffled tones up in the trees?

Not birds: the memory of birds. You are an echo,
only echo, vile feathers, turbid slag, a deaf and lifeless matter
I hold here in my hands. To kiss an ash
is not to give a kiss to love. To bite a withered branch
is not to place those shining lips upon a breast
whose tepid turgidity should shed its light upon those teeth
that gleam with ivory sheen. The sun, the sun is dazzling!

Pull apart the rustling gown, the useless final trappings
of the city. Strip to nakedness
the flowing spring, the glowing body
where fervent life stirs among the branches,
tropical and seared with heat, that an equator thrusts.

Drink, drink the spent passion of a noonday
that at its zenith spews out its light and engulfs you
in its fiery breath and melts you. Vibrant, lovely death,
embers of the day! Virgin forests that destroy themselves in flames!

NO ESTRELLA

¿Quién dijo que ese cuerpo
tallado a besos, brilla
resplandeciente en astro
feliz? ¡Ah, estrella mía,
desciende! Aquí en la hierba
sea cuerpo al fin, sea carne
tu luz. Te tenga al cabo,
latiendo entre los juncos,
estrella derribada
que dé su sangre o brillos
para mi amor. ¡Ah, nunca
inscrita arriba! Humilde,
tangible, aquí la tierra
te espera. Un hombre te ama.

NO STAR

Who said that a body
carved from kisses shines
resplendently, an orb
of happiness? Oh star of mine,
descend! May your light finally
be flesh, be body, here upon
the grass. May I at last
possess you, throbbing in the reeds,
star fallen to the earth,
who for my love would sacrifice
your blood or gleam. No, never,
heavenly one! Here, humble
and tangible, the earth awaits you.
Here, a man loves you.

EL DESNUDO

I

¿Qué llevas ahí, en tu gracioso cesto de margaritas ligeras?
El poniente sin mancha quiere besarme desde tus mejillas inocentes.
Un cándido corpiño encierra la gloria dulce de un mediodía
    prisionero,
mientras tu cuello erguido sostiene la crespa concentración de la luz,
sobre la que los pájaros virginales se encienden.

Pero suelta, suelta tu gracioso cestillo,
mágica mensajera de los campos:
échate sobre el césped aquí a la orilla del río.
Y déjame que en tu oído yo musite mi sombra,
mi penumbrosa esperanza bajo los álamos plateados.

II

Acerca ahora tus pies desnudos,
húndelos en el agua.
Un hervor de oro, de carmín, de plata rápida,
cruza ligero, confundiendo su instantáneo fulgor
con tu espuma constante, oh rosa.
Déjame ahora beber ese agua pura,
besar acaso ciegamente
unos pétalos frescos, un tallo erguido,
un perfume mojado a primavera,
mientras tu cuerpo hermoso arriba orea
su cabello luciente y tus dos manos ríen
entre su luz, y tu busto palpita.

NUDE

I

What are you carrying there, in your elegant basket of graceful
    daisies?
The untainted setting sun yearns to kiss me from your unblemished
    cheeks.
A glowing bodice enfolds the tender glory of a captive noon,
while your throat held high sustains the thick-set tresses of the light
above which virgin birds burst into flame.

Put down your elegant basket, set it down,
that magic messenger from the fields;
lie down by the river's edge here on the grass.
And let me whisper in your ear my dark despair,
my penumbral hope beneath the silver poplar trees.

II

Bring close your naked feet,
thrust them in the water.
A swirl of gold, of crimson, of fleeting silver
sweeps across the sky, confounding all its instant radiance
with your unchanging foam, oh rose.
Let me now drink that crystal water,
and perhaps blindly kiss
some newly blossomed petals, a tall straight stem,
a perfume steeped in spring,
while overhead your comely body airs
its shining tresses and your two hands laugh
amidst its light, and your bosom throbs.

III

Tu desnudo mojado no teme a la luz.
Todo el verde paisaje se hace más tierno
en presencia de tu cuerpo extendido.
Sobre tu seno alerta un pájaro rumoroso
viene a posar su canción, y se yergue.
Sobre la trémula cima su garganta extasiada
canta a la luz, y siente dulce tu calor propagándole.
Mira un instante la tibia llanura aún húmeda del rocío
y con su lento pico amoroso bebe,
bebe la perlada claridad de tu cuerpo,
alzando al cielo su plumada garganta,
ebrio de amor, de luz, de claridad, de música.

IV

Mirar anochecer tu cuerpo desnudo,
goteante todavía del día,
sobre el césped tranquilo, en la mágica atmósfera del amor.
Con mi dedo he trazado sobre tu carne
unas tristes palabras de despedida.
Tu seno aterciopelado silencia mi caricia postrera:
ya casi tu corazón se para.
En tu cuello una música se ensordece,
mudo gemido del poniente anhelante,
y si te miro veo la luz, la luz última
sin sangre, extinguirse en un gran grito final contra mis ojos, ciega.

Súbitamente me hundo en tu boca
y allí bebo todo el último estertor de la noche.

III

Your wet naked figure has no fear of light.
All the landscape's green becomes more tender
in the presence of your outstretched body.
On your wakeful breast, a trilling bird
comes to offer its song, and swells with pride.
Atop that height, its full ecstatic voice
sings to the light and feels your tender warmth disseminate him.
He looks a moment at the tepid plain still humid with dew
and with his slow amorous beak he drinks,
drinks the pearly brightness of your flesh,
raising toward the sky his feathered throat,
drunk with love, with light, with radiance, with melody.

IV

Behold your naked body turn to night,
still wet with moisture of the day,
upon the tranquil meadow in the magic atmosphere of love.
With my finger I have traced upon your flesh
some sad words of farewell.
Your velutinous breast silences my last caress:
your heart has almost ceased to beat.
In your throat a melody falls still,
mute lamentation of the panting western wind,
and if I look at you I see the light, the dying light,
now drained of blood, expiring in a final cry before my eyes, blinded.

Suddenly I plunge into your mouth
and drink there all the last death rattle of the night.

EL CUERPO Y EL ALMA

Pero es más triste todavía, mucho más triste.
Triste como la rama que deja caer su fruto para nadie.
Más triste, más. Como ese vaho
que de la tierra exhala después la pulpa muerta.
Como esa mano que del cuerpo tendido
se eleva y quiere solamente acariciar las luces,
la sonrisa doliente, la noche aterciopelada y muda.
Luz de la noche sobre el cuerpo tendido sin alma.
Alma fuera, alma fuera del cuerpo, planeando
tan delicadamente sobre la triste forma abandonada.
Alma de niebla dulce, suspendida
sobre su ayer amante, cuerpo inerme
que pálido se enfría con las nocturnas horas
y queda quieto, solo, dulcemente vacío.

Alma de amor que vela y se separa
vacilando, y al fin se aleja tiernamente fría.

THE BODY AND THE SOUL

But it is even sadder still, much sadder.
As sad as the bough that drops its fruit for no one.
Much, much sadder. Like the mist
that from the ground the dead fruit then exhales.
Like the hand that from the outstretched body
rises and wants only to caress the lights,
the dolorous smile, the mute and velvety night.
Light of the night above the outstretched soulless body.
The soul outside, soul outside the body, gliding
in delicate flight above the sad abandoned form.
Soul of gentle mist, suspended
above yesterday's lover, a defenseless body
now pale cools off in the hours of the night
and lies there quiet, alone and gently empty.

Soul of love that holds vigil but is reluctant
to depart, and at last withdraws tenderly cold.

LA ROSA

Yo sé que aquí en mi mano
te tengo, rosa fría.
Desnudo el rayo débil
del sol te alcanza. Hueles,
emanas. ¿Desde dónde,
trasunto helado que hoy
me mientes? ¿Desde un reino
secreto de hermosura,
donde tu aroma esparces
para invadir un cielo
total en que dichosos
tus solos aires, fuegos,
perfumes se respiran?
¡Ah, sólo allí celestes
criaturas tú embriagas!

Pero aquí, rosa fría,
secreta estás, inmóvil;
menuda rosa pálida
que en esta mano finges
tu imagen en la tierra.

THE ROSE

I know that here I hold you
in my very hand, cold rose.
The naked fragile beam of sunlight
reaches out to you. Your fragrance,
your aromas emanate. Where
do you come from, frozen image
that today deceives me?
From some secret kingdom far
where only beauty reigns, where you
exude sweet scents that penetrate
a total sky in which the very
heavens breathe your airs and fires,
your rare and unexcelled perfumes?
Celestial creatures, there alone
can you indulge your ecstasies!

But here below, cold rose, you guard
your secret, mute, immutable,
diminutive and soft pale rose
that in this hand of mine pretends
to be your image on this earth.

LAS MANOS

Mira tu mano, que despacio se mueve,
transparente, tangible, atravesada por la luz,
hermosa, viva, casi humana en la noche.
Con reflejo de luna, con color de mejilla, con vaguedad de sueño
mírala así crecer, mientras alzas el brazo,
búsqueda inútil de una noche perdida,
ala de luz que cruzando en silencio
toca carnal esa bóveda oscura.

No fosforece tu pesar, no ha atrapado
ese caliente palpitar de otro vuelo.
Mano volante perseguida: pareja.
Dulces, oscuras, apagadas, cruzáis.

Sois las amantes vocaciones, los signos
que en la tiniebla sin sonido se apelan.
Cielo extinguido de luceros que, tibio,
campo a los vuelos silenciosos te brindas.
Manos de amantes que murieron, recientes,
manos con vida que volantes se buscan
y cuando chocan y se estrechan encienden
sobre los hombres una luna instantánea.

HANDS

Look at your hand that slowly moves,
transparent, tangible, traversed by light,
lovely, vital, all but human in the night.
With the moon's reflection, with the color of a cheek, with the
    vagueness of a dream,
look at how it grows as you raise your arm,
in useless quest for a night now lost,
a wing of light in silent crossing
touches carnally that darkened vault.

Your sorrow does not phosphoresce, nor has it caught
that heated palpitation of another flight.
Persecuted, soaring hand: you form a pair.
Tender, dark, extinguished, you traverse the sky.

You are love's callings, the symbols
that in the noiseless dark call to one another.
Sky now tepid and devoid of stars offers its
ample field for all your silent flights.
The hands of lovers who have lately died,
hands with life that soaring seek their mate
and as they collide and embrace, they ignite
above man's head an instantaneous moon.

LOS BESOS

Sólo eres tú, continua,
graciosa, quien se entrega,
quien hoy me llama. Toma,
toma el calor, la dicha,
la cerrazón de bocas
selladas. Dulcemente
vivimos. Muere, ríndete.
Sólo los besos reinan:
sol tibio y amarillo,
riente, delicado,
que aquí muere, en las bocas
felices, entre nubes
rompientes, entre azules
dichosos, donde brillan
los besos, las delicias
de la tarde, la cima
de este poniente loco,
quietísimo, que vibra
y muere. —Muere, sorbe
la vida. —Besa. —Beso.
¡Oh mundo así dorado!

KISSES

It is you alone, continuous,
of comely grace who give yourself
and call to me today. Accept,
accept the warmth, the happiness,
the closed and cloudy dark of mouths
tight-sealed. In gentle manner
we have lived. Die, surrender.
Nothing more than kisses reign:
a waning, tepid yellow sun
that smiling, fragile, delicate,
here in the happy mouths expires,
between the stormy clouds that break,
between the radiant, joyous blues
where kisses shine, the evening's
glad delights, the dazzling summit
of this eccentric setting sun,
so very quiet now, that pulses
in the west and dies. —Die, absorb
life's fullness. —Kiss me! —Thee I kiss.
Oh glowing world thus touched with gold!

3

PRIMAVERA EN LA TIERRA

Vosotros fuisteis,
espíritus de un alto cielo,
poderes benévolos que presidisteis mi vida,
iluminando mi frente en los feraces días de la alegría juvenil.

Amé, amé la dichosa Primavera
bajo el signo divino de vuestras alas levísimas,
oh poderosos, oh extensos dueños de la tierra.
Desde un alto cielo de gloria,
espíritus celestes, vivificadores del hombre,
iluminasteis mi frente con los rayos vitales de un sol que llenaba
    la tierra de sus totales cánticos.

Todo el mundo creado
resonaba con la amarilla gloria
de la luz cambiante.
Pájaros de colores,
con azules y rojas y verdes y amatistas,
coloreadas alas con plumas como el beso,
saturaban la bóveda palpitante de dicha,
batiente como seno, como plumaje o seno,
como la piel turgente que los besos tiñeran.

Los árboles saturados colgaban
densamente cargados de una savia encendida.
Flores pujantes, hálito repentino de una tierra gozosa,
abrían su misterio, su boca suspirante,
labios rojos que el sol dulcemente quemaba.

SPRINGTIME ON THE EARTH

You it was,
the spirits of a lofty sky,
benevolent powers who have ruled my life,
in those fertile days of youthful happiness that lit up my brow.

I loved, I dearly loved the radiant Spring
beneath the hallowed symbol of your fleet and agile wings,
oh powerful, extensive masters of the earth.
From a lofty sky of glory,
celestial spirits, you who first gave life to man,
you lit up my brow with vital rays of sun that with its total canticles
    filled all the earth.

The whole created world
resounded with the yellow glory
of the changing light.
Birds of many hues,
of blues and reds, greens and amethysts,
the multicolored wings with feathers like a kiss,
saturated with happiness the sky's palpitating dome,
beating like a breast, like feathers or a breast,
like the turgid flesh that kisses tinged with color.

The saturated limbs of trees
hung heavy-burdened with a fiery sap.
The sprouting flowers, of a joyous earth the sudden breath,
spread wide their mystery, their sighing mouth,
red lips the sun had gently set aflame.

Todo abría su cáliz bajo la luz caliente.

Las grandes rocas, casi de piedra o carne,
se amontonaban sobre dulces montañas,
que reposaban cálidas como cuerpos cansados
de gozar una hermosa sensualidad luciente.
Las aguas vivas, espumas del amor en los cuerpos,
huían, se atrevían, se rozaban, cantaban.
Risas frescas los bosques enviaban, ya mágicos;
atravesados sólo de un atrevido viento.

Pero vosotros, dueños fáciles de la vida,
presidisteis mi juventud primera.
Un muchacho desnudo, cubierto de vegetal alegría,
huía por las arenas vívidas del amor
hacia el gran mar extenso,
hacia la vasta inmensidad derramada
que melodiosamente pide un amor consumado.

La gran playa marina,
no abanico, no rosa, no vara de nardo,
pero concha de un nácar irisado de ardores,
se extendía vibrando, resonando, cantando,
poblada de unos pájaros de virginal blancura.

Un rosa cándido por las nubes remotas
evocaba mejillas recientes donde un beso
ha teñido purezas de magnolia mojada,

Beneath the warming light, all nature opened up its calyx.

Massive rocks, almost of stone or flesh,
piled one atop the other on the gentle mountain slopes
that lay still warm like bodies spent
indulging in a fair resplendent sensuality.
Living waters, spumes of love on bodies,
fled, became more daring, touched one another, sang.
The forests, magic now, set forth cool laughter;
traversed by nothing but a daring wind.

But you, life's gentle masters,
were the ruling spirit of my early years.
A naked youth, enrobed in floral happiness,
fled through the vivid sands of love
toward the great expansive sea,
toward the vast immensity that overflows
and asks with voice of melody for love's fulfillment.

The ocean's lengthy shore
was neither open fan, nor rose, nor spikenard's bough,
but shell of a nacre bright with zeal
stretched pulsing, resonating, singing there,
its only population birds of virgin white.

Through the distant clouds a shining rose
conjured up cherubic cheeks of which a kiss
has left the tinted purities of moist magnolia,

ojos húmedos, frente salina y alba
y un rubio pelo que en el ocaso ondea.

Pero el mar se irisaba. Sus verdes cambiantes,
sus azules lucientes, su resonante gloria
clamaba erguidamente hasta los puros cielos,
emergiendo entre espumas su vasta voz amante.

En ese mar alzado, gemidor, que dolía
como una piedra toda de luz que a mí me amase,
mojé mis pies, herí con mi cuerpo sus ondas,
y dominé insinuando mi bulto afiladísimo,
como un delfín que goza las espumas tendidas.

Gocé, sufrí, encendí los agoniosos mares,
los abrasados mares,
y sentí la pujanza de la vida cantando,
ensalzado en el ápice del placer a los cielos.

Siempre fuisteis, oh dueños poderosos,
los dispensadores de todas las gracias,
tutelares hados eternos que presidisteis la fiesta de la vida
que yo viví como criatura entre todas.

Los árboles, las espumas, las flores, los abismos,
como las rocas y aves y las aguas fugaces,

humid eyes, a white and saline brow,
and fair blond locks that in the sunset undulate.

But the sea was iridescent. Its changing greens,
its shining blues and resonating glory
clamored proudly to the clear blue skies,
its vast love-filled voice emerging from the foam.

In the roiling, wailing sea that grieved
like a stone all of light tendering me its love,
I wet my feet, I thrust my body through its waves,
I overcame her with my slender, sharpened form,
like a dolphin taking pleasure in the spacious foam.

I enjoyed, I suffered, I set the anguished seas afire,
the burning seas,
and felt the pulsing drive of life's singing,
extolling the heavens at the apex of its pleasure.

You, oh mighty masters, always were
the dispensers of all graces,
the eternal guiding spirits who presided at the feast of life
that I experienced, one creature among all.

Trees, spumes, flowers, and abysses,
like rocks and birds and flowing waters,

todo supo de vuestra presencia invisible
en el mundo que yo viví en los alegres días juveniles.

Hoy que la nieve también existe bajo vuestra presencia,
miro los cielos de plomo pesaroso
y diviso los hierros de las torres que elevaron los hombres
como espectros de todos los deseos efímeros.

Y miro las vagas telas que los hombres ofrecen,
máscaras que no lloran sobre las ciudades cansadas,
mientras siento lejana la música de los sueños
en que escapan las flautas de la Primavera apagándose.

everything responded to your unseen presence
in the world which I inhabited in those happy youthful days.

Today, when snow also exists beneath your presence,
I behold the heavens with their leaden weight
and I discern the iron of towers men have raised
that stand like ghosts of all ephemeral desire.

And I behold the vague uncertain canvases that men hold out,
the masks that do not weep above the weary cities,
and I sense the far-off music of dreams
in which the flutes of Spring expire and fade away.

CASI ME AMABAS

Alma celeste para amar nacida.
ESPRONCEDA

Casi me amabas.
Sonreías, con tu gran pelo rubio donde la luz resbala hermosamente.
Ante tus manos el resplandor del día se aplacaba continuo,
dando distancia a tu cuerpo perfecto.
La transparencia alegre de la luz no ofendía,
pero doraba dulce tu claridad indemne.
Casi . . ., casi me amabas.

Yo llegaba de allí, de más allá, de esa oscura conciencia
de tierra, de un verdear sombrío de selvas fatigadas,
donde el viento caducó para las rojas músicas;
donde las flores no se abrían cada mañana celestemente
ni donde el vuelo de las aves hallaba al amanecer virgen el día.

Un fondo marino te rodeaba.
Una concha de nácar intacta bajo tu pie, te ofrece
a ti como la última gota de una espuma marina.
Casi . . ., casi me amabas.

¿Por qué viraste los ojos, virgen de las entrañas del mundo
que esta tarde de primavera
pones frialdad de luna sobre la luz del día
y como un disco de castidad sin noche,
huyes rosada por un azul virgíneo?

YOU ALMOST LOVED ME

Celestial soul that for love was born.
ESPRONCEDA

You almost loved me.
You were smiling, you with your great blond wreath of hair on
    which the light so gracefully cascades.
Before your hands, the brilliance of the day grew ever softer,
making your perfect figure seem farther away.
The happy transparency of light did not offend me,
for it gently tinged with gold your unscathed clarity.
You almost . . ., almost loved me.

From far off I came, from far beyond, from that dark memory
of earth, of the darkling green of weary jungles,
where the wind brought to an end your ruby melodies;
where flowers did not open every morning in the sky
and where no flights of birds at dawn found the day still virgin.

An expanse of sea encircled you.
A shell of nacre beneath your foot offers to you
what seems the final drop of foam spewed by the sea.
You almost . . ., almost loved me.

Why did you avert your eyes, virgin from the entrails of the earth,
you who on this afternoon in spring
place moonlight's chill against the light of day,
and like a disk of chastity that knows no night,
flee rose-colored through a virginal blue?

Tu escorzo dulce de pensativa rosa sin destino
mira hacia el mar. ¿Por qué, por qué ensordeces
y ondeante al viento tu cabellera, intentas
mentir los rayos de tu lunar belleza?

¡Si tú me amabas como la luz! . . . No escapes,
mate, insensible, crepuscular, sellada.
Casi, casi me amaste. Sobre las ondas puras
del mar sentí tu cuerpo como estelar espuma,
caliente, vivo, propagador. El beso
no, no, no fue de luz: palabras
nobles sonaron: me prometiste el mundo
recóndito, besé tu aliento, mientras la crespa ola
quebró en mis labios, y como playa tuve
todo el calor de tu hermosura en brazos.

Sí, sí, me amaste sobre los brillos, fija,
final, extática. El mar inmóvil
detuvo entonces su permanente aliento,
y vi en los cielos resplandecer la luna,
feliz, besada, y revelarme el mundo.

Your sweet foreshortened figure of pensive rose foredoomed
looks out toward the sea. Why, why do you fall silent
and, loosing to the wind your cascading hair, attempt
to counterfeit your lunar beauty's beams?

If you once loved me like the light! . . . Don't run from me,
lusterless, unfeeling, crepuscular, closed tight.
You almost, almost loved me. Above the sea's pure waves
I sensed your body like a spume of stars,
warm, living, procreant. The kiss
was not, not, not of light: noble words
were said: you promised me the hidden
world, I kissed your breath, as the curling wave
broke on my lips, and like a beach I held
all of your beauty's warmth within my arms.

Yes, yes, you loved me above the luster, fixed,
final and ecstatic. The unmoving sea
then ceased its constant breathing,
and in the heavens I saw a glimmer of the moon,
joyful, kissed, and it revealed the world to me.

LOS POETAS

¿Los poetas, preguntas?

Yo vi una flor quebrada
por la brisa. El clamor
silencioso de pétalos
cayendo arruinados
de sus perfectos sueños.
¡Vasto amor sin delirio
bajo la luz volante,
mientras los ojos miran
un temblor de palomas
que una asunción inscriben!
Yo vi, yo vi otras alas.
Vastas alas dolidas.
Ángeles desterrados
de su celeste origen
en la tierra dormían
su paraíso excelso.
Inmensos sueños duros
todavía vigentes
se adivinaban sólidos
en su frente blanquísima.
¿Quién miró aquellos mundos,
isla feraz de un sueño,
pureza diamantina
donde el amor combate?
¿Quién vio nubes volando,

POETS

And poets, you inquire?

I saw a flower broken
by the breeze. The silent
clamor of petals falling
into the destruction
of their perfect dreams.
Vast love without delirium
beneath the soaring light,
as my eyes behold the tremor,
the shuddering of doves
writing an assumption there!
I saw, I saw still other wings.
Vast grieving wings.
Angels banished from
their celestial origins
now bound to earth must seek
their lofty paradise in sleep.
Immense harsh dreams
retaining still their force
could on white and shining brows
in solid magnitude be seen.
Who could perceive those worlds,
the fertile island of a dream,
the diamantine purity
where love is locked in combat?
Who saw clouds in flight,

brazos largos, las flores,
las caricias, la noche
bajo los pies, la luna
como un seno pulsando?
Ángeles sin descanso
tiñen sus alas lúcidas
de un rubor sin crepúsculo,
entre los valles verdes.
Un amor, mediodía,
vertical se desploma
permanente en los hombros
desnudos del amante.
Las muchachas son ríos
felices; sus espumas
—manos continuas— atan
a los cuellos las flores
de una luz suspirada
entre hermosas palabras.
Los besos, los latidos,
las aves silenciosas,
todo está allá, en los senos
secretísimos, duros,
que sorprenden continuos
a unos labios eternos.
¡Qué tierno acento impera
en los bosques sin sombras,
donde las suaves pieles,

long arms, the flowers,
caresses and the night
underfoot, the moon
palpitating like a breast?
Angels ever wakeful
color their lucid wings
with blushes no twilight shades
below in greening valleys.
Love, high noon, comes
plunging down forever
on the naked shoulders
of the beloved below.
Young girls are rivers
full of joy; their spume
—eternal hands—fasten
round their necks flowers
that a lightbeam sighed
between exquisite words.
Kisses and heartbeats,
hushed and silent birds,
everything is there,
in hard, secretive breasts
that continually surprise
pairs of eternal lips.
What tender voices reign there
in forests without shadow
where the gentle flesh,

la gacela sin nombre,
un venado dulcísimo,
levanta su respuesta
sobre su frente al día!
¡Oh, misterio del aire
que se enreda en los bultos
inexplicablemente,
como espuma sin dueño!
Ángeles misteriosos,
humano ardor, erigen
cúpulas pensativas
sobre las frescas ondas.
Sus alas laboriosas
mueven un viento esquivo,
que abajo roza frentes
amorosas del aire.
Y la tierra sustenta
pies desnudos, columnas
que el amor ensalzara,
templos de dicha fértil,
que la luna revela.
Cuerpos, almas o luces
repentinas, que cantan
cerca del mar, en liras
casi celestes, solas.

the gazelle unnamed,
a deer so very gentle,
lifts upon its fragile brow
its solemn answer to the day.
Oh, what mystery of air
inexplicably entwining
with great vague shapes
like seaspume with no master!
Mysterious angels,
human ardor, raise
their pensive cupolas
above the cooling waves.
Their never-idle wings
set astir an elusive wind
that gently touches here below
brows enamored of the air.
And the earth sustains
discalced feet, columns raised
by love exalted,
temples of fertile joy
that the moon reveals.
Bodies, souls or lights
suddenly appear and sing
beside the sea in lyrics
almost celestial, sing alone.

¿Quién vio ese mundo sólido,
quién batió con sus plumas
ese viento radiante
que en unos labios muere
dando vida a los hombres?
¿Qué legión misteriosa,
ángeles en destierro,
continuamente llega,
invisible a los ojos?
No, no preguntes; calla.
La ciudad, sus espejos,
su voz blanca, su fría
crueldad sin sepulcro,
desconoce esas alas.

Tú preguntas, preguntas . . .

Who has beheld that solid world,
who with feathered plume
whipped the radiant wind,
which expires on paired lips
conferring life on man?
What mysterious legion,
angels long in exile,
continuously arrives,
invisible to the eye?
No, do not ask; be silent.
The city, its mirrors,
its empty voice, its cold
and tombless cruelty
repudiates those wings.

You inquire, inquire . . .

LUNA DEL PARAÍSO

Símbolo de la luz tú fuiste,
oh luna, en las nocturnas horas coronadas.
Tu pálido destello,
con el mismo fulgor que una muda inocencia,
aparecía cada noche presidiendo mi dicha,
callando tiernamente sobre mis frescas horas.

Un azul grave, pleno, serenísimo,
te ofrecía su seno generoso
para tu alegre luz, oh luna joven,
y tú tranquila, esbelta, resbalabas
con un apenas insinuado ademán de silencio.

¡Plenitud de tu estancia en los cielos completos!
No partida por la tristeza,
sino suavemente rotunda, liminar, perfectísima,
yo te sentía en breve como dos labios dulces
y sobre mi frente oreada de los vientos clementes
sentía tu llamamiento juvenil, tu posada ternura.

No era dura la tierra. Mis pasos resbalaban
como mudas palabras sobre un césped amoroso.
Y en la noche estelar, por los aires, tus ondas
volaban, convocaban, musitaban, querían.

MOON OF PARADISE

Symbol of light you were,
oh moon, in the crowning hours of night.
Your pallid wake,
with the same splendor as a mute innocence,
appeared each night, the guardian of my happiness,
tenderly passing in silence above my cool fresh hours.

A solemn, full, and tranquil blue
held out to you its ample bosom
for your happy light, oh youthful moon,
and you, in lithe tranquillity slipped by
with a movement barely perceived, of silence.

Fullness of your presence in the perfect skies!
By sorrow unperturbed,
how suavely round and full, beginning, perfect there,
I felt you afterwards like two soft lips
and on my forehead cooled by clement winds
I sensed your youthful call, your settled tenderness.

It was not hard, the earth. My steps would glide along
like muted words upon a loving stretch of lawn.
And in the star-swept night, through the air, your waves
took flight, beckoned me, whispered and desired.

¡Cuánto te amé en las sombras! Cuando aparecías en el monte,
en aquel monte tibio, carnal bajo tu celo,
tu ojo lleno de sapiencia velaba
sobre mi ingenua sangre tendida en las laderas.
Y cuando de mi aliento ascendía el más gozoso cántico
hasta mí el río encendido me acercaba tus gracias.

Entre las frondas de los pinos oscuros
mudamente vertías tu tibieza invisible,
y el ruiseñor silencioso sentía su garganta desatarse de amor
si en sus plumas un beso de tus labios dejabas.

Tendido sobre el césped vibrante,
¡cuántas noches cerré mis ojos bajo tus dedos blandos,
mientras en mis oídos el mágico pájaro nocturno
se derretía en el más dulce frenesí musical!

Toda tu luz velaba sobre aquella cálida bola de pluma
que te cantaba a ti, luna bellísima,
enterneciendo a la noche con su ardiente entusiasmo,
mientras tú siempre dulce, siempre viva, enviabas
pálidamente tus luces sin sonido.

En otras noches, cuando el amor presidía mi dicha,
un bulto claro de una muchacha apacible,
desnudo sobre el césped era hermoso paisaje.
Y sobre su carne celeste, sobre su fulgor rameado
besé tu luz, blanca luna ciñéndola.

How deeply I loved you in the shadows! When you appeared on the
    mountain,
that tepid mountain, sensual beneath your passion,
your all-knowing eye kept watch
above my guileless blood stretched across the slopes.
And when the happiest of canticles ascended from my breath,
the river all inflamed brought your gracious beauty to my side.

Among the dark pine's leaves
you quietly poured out your unseen warmth,
and the silent nightingale could feel his throat burst with love
if from your lips you left a kiss upon his plumage.

Lying there upon the vibrant grass,
how many nights I closed my eyes beneath your gentle fingers,
while in my ears the magic bird of night
would melt into the sweetest frenzy of song!

All my light kept watch above the fervent globe of feathers
as it sang its song to you, most lovely moon,
moving to compassion with its ardent zeal the very night,
while you, ever gentle, ever living,
palely emitted your soundless light.

Other nights, when love ruled my happiness,
the limpid figure of a peaceful girl,
nude upon the gentle lawn, became a lovely landscape.
And above her celestial flesh, above her leafy brilliancy,
I kissed your light, white moon embracing her.

Mis labios en su garganta bebían tu brillo, agua pura, luz pura;
en su cintura estreché tu espuma fugitiva,
y en sus senos sentí tu nacimiento tras el monte incendiado,
pulidamente bella sobre su piel erguida.

Besé sobre su cuerpo tu rubor, y en los labios,
roja luna, naciste, redonda, iluminada,
luna estrellada por mi beso, luna húmeda
que una secreta luz interior me cediste.

Yo no tuve palabras para el amor. Los cabellos
acogieron mi boca como los rayos tuyos.
En ellos yo me hundí, yo me hundí preguntando
si eras tú ya mi amor, si me oías besándote.

Cerré los ojos una vez más y tu luz límpida,
tu luz inmaculada me penetró nocturna.
Besando el puro rostro, yo te oí ardientes voces,
dulces palabras que tus rayos cedían,
y sentí que mi sangre, en tu luz convertida,
recorría mis venas destellando en la noche.

Noches tuyas, luna total: ¡oh luna, luna entera!
Yo te amé en los felices días coronados.
Y tú, secreta luna, luna mía,
fuiste presente en la tierra, en mis brazos humanos.

My lips against her throat drank in your gleam, pure water, pure light;
around her waist I pressed your fleeting spray,
and between her breasts I felt your nativity behind the blazing
    mountain,
in spotless beauty above her risen flesh.

I kissed your blushing glow upon her body, and on her lips,
red moon, you were born, full-rounded, full of light,
a moon enshrined in stars by my kiss, a humid moon
that yielded up to me a secret inner light.

I had no words of love to say. Her long tresses
fell upon my mouth like rays of yours.
I dove into them, dove still asking
if you had now become my love, if you could hear me kissing you.

Once more I closed my eyes and your limpid light,
your light immaculate and nocturnal pierced me.
As I kissed your perfect face, I heard your ardent cries,
the gentle words of love your beams conveyed,
and I felt that my blood, transformed into your light,
was running through my veins and sparkling in the night.

The nights were yours, rounded moon: oh moon, perfect moon!
I loved you in the happy final days.
And you, a secret moon, moon of mine,
you were a presence on the earth, here in my human arms.

HIJO DEL SOL

La luz, la hermosa luz del Sol,
cruel envío de un imposible,
dorado anuncio de un fuego hurtado al hombre,
envía su fulgurante promesa arrebatada,
siempre, siempre en el cielo, serenamente estático.

Tú serías, tu lumbre empírea,
carbón para el destino quemador de unos labios,
sello indeleble a una inmortalidad convocada,
sonando en los oídos de un hombre alzado a un mito.

¡Oh estrellas, oh luceros! Constelación eterna
salvada al fin de un sufrimiento terreno,
bañándose en un mar constante y puro.
Tan infinitamente,
sobrevivirías, tan alto,
hijo del Sol, hombre al fin rescatado,
sublime luz creadora, hijo del universo,
derramando tu sonido estelar, tu sangre-mundos.

¡Oh Sol, Sol mío!

Pero el Sol no reparte
sus dones:
da sólo sombras,
sombras, espaldas de una luz engañosa,

CHILD OF THE SUN

The light, the beautiful light of the Sun,
cruel remittance of an impossible being,
golden harbinger of a fire stolen from man,
sent forth its rash and fulgurating promise,
forever and forever in the serene, ecstatic sky.

You would be, your empyrean flame would be,
the firebrand for the burning destiny of lips,
indelible symbol that an immortality convoked,
ringing in the ears of man now raised to myth.

Stars, oh lovely stars! Eternal constellation
delivered from an earthly suffering at last,
bathing in a pure and constant sea.
So infinitely
and so high above, you would survive,
child of the Sun, man at last redeemed,
sublime creative light, child of the universe,
pouring down your starry sound, your blood of worlds.

Oh Sun, my very Sun!

But the Sun does not allot
its gifts:
it gives only shadows,
shadows, reversals of deceitful light,

sombras frías, dolientes muros para unos labios
hechos para ti, Sol, para tu lumbre en tacto.

Yo te veo, hermosísimo,
amanecer cada día,
sueño de una mente implacable,
dorado Sol para el que yo nací como todos los hombres,
para abrasarme en tu lumbre corpórea,
combustible de carne hecho ya luz, luz sólo, en tu pira de fuego.

Sólo así viviría . . .

Pero te miro ascender lentamente,
fulgurando tu mentida promesa,
convocando tan dulce sobre mi carne el tibio
calor, tu hálito mágico,
mientras mis brazos alzo tendidos en el aire.

Pero nunca te alcanzo, boca ardiente,
pecho de luz contra mi pecho todo,
destino mío inmortal donde entregarme
a la muerte abrasante hecho chispas perdidas.

Devuelto así por tu beso a los espacios,
a las estrellas, oh sueño primaveral de un fuego célico.
Devuelto en brillos dulces, en veladora promesa,
en ya eterna belleza del amor, con descanso.

cold shadows, grieving walls for lips
made for you, Sun, for your all-embracing light.

I see you in all your beauty
as you dawn each day,
the dream of a relentless mind,
the golden Sun for which, as all men were, I too was born,
born to be ignited in your corporeal fire,
fuel of flesh made light and only light upon your pyre of flame.

Thus only would I live . . .

But I behold your slow ascent,
shining with mendacious promise,
gently summoning upon my flesh the quiet
warmth, your magic breath,
as I lift my arms and stretch them in the air.

But I never quite possess you, ardent mouth,
breast of light pressed tightly to my breast,
immortal destiny of mine in which I give myself
to all-consuming death now turned to dying embers.

Thus by your kiss returned to the vastnesses of space,
to the very stars, oh spring night's dream of heaven's fire.
Returned in gentle brilliances, in watchful promise,
in the now eternal beauty, in the restfulness of love.

COMO SERPIENTE

Miré tus ojos sombríos bajo el cielo apagado.
Tu frente mate con palidez de escama.
Tu boca, donde un borde morado me estremece.
Tu corazón inmóvil como una piedra oscura.

Te estreché la cintura, fría culebra gruesa que en mis dedos resbala.
Contra mi pecho cálido sentí tu paso lento.
Viscosamente fuiste sólo un instante mía,
y pasaste, pasaste, inexorable y larga.

Te vi después, tus dos ojos brillando
tercamente, tendida sobre el arroyo puro,
beber un cielo inerme, tranquilo, que ofrecía
para tu lengua bífida su virginal destello.

Aún recuerdo ese brillo de tu testa sombría,
negra magia que oculta bajo su crespo acero
la luz nefasta y fría de tus pupilas hondas,
donde un hielo en abismos sin luz subyuga a nadie.

¡A nadie! Sola, aguardas un rostro, otra pupila,
azul, verde, en colores felices que rielen
claramente amorosos bajo la luz del día,
o que revelen dulces la boca para un beso.

LIKE A SERPENT

I watched your somber eyes beneath a darkened sky.
Your ashen forehead with the pallor of scales.
Your mouth with purple lips that make me shudder.
Your heart as unresponsive as a dark stone.

I tightly held your waist, cold thick snake that through my fingers
    slips.
Against the warmness of my chest I felt you slowly slither by.
Viscously for just one moment you were mine,
and then passed on, passed on, inexorable and long.

I saw you afterwards, your two eyes shining
stubbornly, above the crystal stream outstretched,
drinking of the tranquil, inert sky that offered up
to your forked tongue its pristine shining galaxy.

I remember still the brilliance of your shadowed head,
black magic that conceals beneath its curly steel
the cold and baneful light of your deep eyes,
where in lightless voids the ice subdues no one.

No one! Alone you await another face, another eye,
blue or green, in festive colors that shimmer
candidly in love beneath the light of day,
or that reveal lips ready for a kiss.

Pero no. En ese monte pelado, en esa cumbre
pelada, están los árboles pelados que tú ciñes.
¿Silba tu boca cruda, o silba el viento roto?
¿Ese rayo es la ira de la maldad, o es sólo
el cielo que desposa su fuego con la cima?

¿Esa sombra es tu cuerpo que en la tormenta escapa,
herido de la cólera nocturna, en el relámpago,
o es el grito pelado de la montaña, libre,
libre sin ti y ya monda, que fulminada exulta?

But no. On that shorn mountain, on that shorn
pinnacle, there stand the bark-shorn trees that you encoil.
Is that hissing from your raw red mouth or from the ragged wind?
Is this the bolt from evil's ire or is it just
the sky that to the heights its fire conjoins?

Is that shadow your body fleeing in the storm,
wounded by the night's anger, in the lightning flash,
or is it the shorn cry of the mountain, free,
free without you and stripped bare, exulting in the lucent bolt?

MAR DEL PARAÍSO

Heme aquí frente a ti, mar, todavía . . .
Con el polvo de la tierra en mis hombros,
impregnado todavía del efímero deseo apagado del hombre,
heme aquí, luz eterna,
vasto mar sin cansancio,
última expresión de un amor que no acaba,
rosa del mundo ardiente.

Eras tú, cuando niño,
la sandalia fresquísima para mi pie desnudo.
Un albo crecimiento de espumas por mi pierna
me engañara en aquella remota infancia de delicias.
Un sol, una promesa
de dicha, una felicidad humana, una cándida correlación de luz
con mis ojos nativos, de ti, mar, de ti, cielo,
imperaba generosa sobre mi frente deslumbrada
y extendía sobre mis ojos su inmaterial palma alcanzable,
abanico de amor o resplandor continuo
que imitaba unos labios para mi piel sin nubes.

Lejos el rumor pedregoso de los caminos oscuros
donde hombres ignoraban tu fulgor aún virgíneo.
Niño grácil, para mí la sombra de la nube en la playa
no era el torvo presentimiento de mi vida en su polvo,
no era el contorno bien preciso donde la sangre un día

SEA OF PARADISE

Here I am, sea, before you still . . .
With the dust of earth upon my shoulders,
pregnant still with man's extinct ephemeral desire,
here I am, eternal light,
vast sea that knows no rest,
the last expression of a love that never ends,
rose of the world aflame.

You, in my boyhood, were
the fresh cool sandal of my unshod foot.
The white upsurge of foam around my legs
beguiled me in that far-off childhood of delights.
A sun, a promise
of felicity, a human happiness, a candid correlation of the light
with these very eyes, from you, sea, and you, sky,
in noble selflessness held sway above my dazzled brow
and opened out before my eyes its immaterial palm leaf half-perceived,
love's open fan or unremitting radiance
that for my cloudless flesh would masquerade as lips.

Far off the stony sound of darkened roads
where men knew nothing of your still virgin gleam.
Slender child, for me the shadow of a cloud upon the beach
was not the grim foreboding of my life upon its sand,
was not the exacting shape where blood one day

acabaría coagulada, sin destello y sin numen.
Más bien, con mi dedo pequeño, mientras la nube detenía su paso,
yo tracé sobre la fina arena dorada su perfil estremecido,
y apliqué mi mejilla sobre su tierna luz transitoria,
mientras mis labios decían los primeros nombres amorosos:
cielo, arena, mar . . .

El lejano crujir de los aceros, el eco al fondo de los bosques
    partidos por los hombres,
era allí para mí un monte oscuro pero también hermoso.
Y mis oídos confundían el contacto heridor del labio crudo
del hacha en las encinas
con un beso implacable, cierto de amor, en ramas.

La presencia de peces por las orillas, su plata núbil,
el oro no manchado por los dedos de nadie,
la resbalosa escama de la luz, era un brillo en los míos.
No apresé nunca esa forma huidiza de un pez en su hermosura,
la esplendente libertad de los seres,
ni amenacé una vida, porque amé mucho: amaba
sin conocer el amor; sólo vivía . . .

Las barcas que a lo lejos
confundían sus velas con las crujientes alas
de las gaviotas o dejaban espuma como suspiros leves,
hallaban en mi pecho confiado un envío,

would finally coagulate, leaving neither wake nor numen.
Rather, as the cloud stood still, with my small finger
on the fine and golden sand I traced its trembling silhouette,
and held my cheek up to the warm and fleeting light,
while my lips expressed the first names of love:
sky, sand, sea . . .

The distant sound of striking steel, the echo from the depths of
    forests felled by man,
was for me there a dark but splendid wooded height.
And my ears confused the wounding stroke of that crude lip,
the ax's lip against the ilex trees,
with a relentless kiss, made bold by love, upon the boughs.

The presence of fish upon the shores, their silver hues voluptuous,
the gold that no one's fingers yet have stained,
the sleek and slippery scales of light, were on my hands a gleam.
I never captured the fleeting form of a fish in all its beauty,
the resplendent liberty of existing things,
nor have I ever menaced life, for I have greatly loved: I loved
without knowing love; I lived in solitude . . .

The ships whose distant sails
confusedly blended with the whirring wings
of gulls or left behind a foam as soft as sighs,
found in my trusting heart a message sent,

un grito, un nombre de amor, un deseo para mis labios húmedos,
y si las vi pasar, mis manos menudas se alzaron
y gimieron de dicha a su secreta presencia,
ante el azul telón que mis ojos adivinaron,
viaje hacia un mundo prometido, entrevisto,
al que mi destino me convocaba con muy dulce certeza.

Por mis labios de niño cantó la tierra; el mar
cantaba dulcemente azotado por mis manos inocentes.
La luz, tenuamente mordida por mis dientes blanquísimos,
cantó; cantó la sangre de la aurora en mi lengua.

Tiernamente en mi boca, la luz del mundo me iluminaba por dentro.
Toda la asunción de la vida embriagó mis sentidos.
Y los rumorosos bosques me desearon entre sus verdes frondas,
porque la luz rosada era en mi cuerpo dicha.

Por eso hoy, mar,
con el polvo de la tierra en mis hombros,
impregnado todavía del efímero deseo apagado del hombre,
heme aquí, luz eterna,
vasto mar sin cansancio,
rosa del mundo ardiente.
Heme aquí frente a ti, mar, todavía . . .

a cry, a word of love, a longing for my humid lips,
and if I saw them passing by, I'd raise my tiny hands
and moan with happiness before their secret presence,
before that azure canvas that my eyes divined,
a voyage toward a promised world half seen
to which with gentle certainty my destiny had summoned me.

Through my boyish lips the earth broke into song; the sea
sang sweetly, lashed by my innocent hands.
The light, tenuously bitten by my small white teeth
sang out; sang of the blood of dawn reflected on my tongue.

Inside my mouth, with gentle tenderness, the light of the world
    illuminated me within.
All of life's assumption made my senses reel.
And the murmuring forests longed for me among their greening
    boughs,
because inside me the rosy light was happiness.

That is why today, sea,
with the dust of earth upon my shoulders,
pregnant still with man's extinct ephemeral desire,
here I am, eternal light,
vast sea that knows no rest,
rose of the world aflame.
Here I am, sea, before you still . . .

PLENITUD DEL AMOR

¿Qué fresco y nuevo encanto,
qué dulce perfil rubio emerge
de la tarde sin nieblas?
Cuando creí que la esperanza, la ilusión, la vida,
derivaba hacia oriente
en triste y vana busca del placer.
Cuando yo había visto bogar por los cielos
imágenes sonrientes, dulces corazones cansados,
espinas que atravesaban bellos labios,
y un humo casi doliente
donde palabras amantes se deshacían como el aliento del amor sin
    destino . . .
Apareciste tú ligera como el árbol,
como la brisa cálida que un oleaje envía del mediodía, envuelta
en las sales febriles, como en las frescas aguas del azul.

Un árbol joven, sobre un limitado horizonte,
horizonte tangible para besos amantes;
un árbol nuevo y verde que melodiosamente mueve sus hojas
    altaneras
alabando la dicha de su viento en los brazos.

Un pecho alegre, un corazón sencillo como la pleamar remota
que hereda sangre, espuma, de otras regiones vivas.
Un oleaje lúcido bajo el gran sol abierto,
desplegando las plumas de una mar inspirada;
plumas, aves, espumas, mares verdes o cálidas:
todo el mensaje vivo de un pecho rumoroso.

PLENITUDE OF LOVE

What fresh and new enchantment,
what soft blond silhouette emerges
from the mistless afternoon?
When I thought that hope, illusion, life
were all adrift toward the east
in sad and senseless searching for delight.
When I'd seen sailing across the skies
bright shining images, gentle weary hearts,
thorns that pierced through lovely lips,
an almost painful smoky mist
where loving words dissolved like undestined sighs of love . . .
You appeared as light as a tree,
as the torrid breeze sent surging from the noonday sun, immersed
in feverish brines, as in the cooling waters of the blue.

A growing tree, above the limited horizon,
a horizon that a loving kiss could touch;
a new and greening tree, with melodic cadence moves its lofty
    leaves,
reveling in the joy of the wind in its boughs.

A happy breast, a simple heart that like the distant rising tide
inherits blood and foam from other living shores.
A shining swell of wave beneath the great open sun
spreads its feathers of a churning sea;
feathers, birds, and foams, green or torrid seas:
all the living message of a sighing breast.

Yo sé que tu perfil sobre el azul tierno del crepúsculo entero,
no finge vaga nube que un ensueño ha creado.
¡Qué dura frente dulce, qué piedra hermosa y viva,
encendida de besos bajo el sol melodioso,
es tu frente besada por unos labios libres,
rama joven bellísima que un ocaso arrebata!

¡Ah la verdad tangible de un cuerpo estremecido
entre los brazos vivos de tu amante furioso,
que besa vivos labios, blancos dientes, ardores
y un cuello como un agua cálidamente alerta!

Por un torso desnudo tibios hilillos ruedan.
¡Qué gran risa de lluvia sobre tu pecho ardiente!
¡Qué fresco vientre terso, donde su curva oculta
leve musgo de sombra rumoroso de peces!

Muslos de tierra, barcas donde bogar un día
por el músico mar del amor enturbiado
donde escapar libérrimos rumbo a los cielos altos
en que la espuma nace de dos cuerpos volantes.

¡Ah, maravilla lúcida de tu cuerpo cantando,
destellando de besos sobre tu piel despierta:
bóveda centelleante, nocturnamente hermosa,
que humedece mi pecho de estrellas o de espumas!

I know that high above the tender blue of twilight's breadth, your
    silhouette
does not pretend to be a formless cloud that a dream created.
What a hard tender brow, what a beautiful and living stone,
ignited by the kisses of a warm melodic sun,
is your brow that has been kissed by daring lips,
a beautiful and youthful bough that a sunset violates!

What substantial truth this trembling body has
in the living arms of your impassioned lover,
he who kisses living lips, white teeth, fervors
and a throat like warmly rushing water!

Around a naked torso tepid threads of water run.
What a joyous burst of rain upon your ardent breast!
What a cool silken stomach, where its curving arch conceals
a fragile moss of shadows that is resonant of fish!

Thighs of earth, ships in which one day we rowed
across a deep-throated sea of turbid love
and where we fled in perfect freedom toward the heaven's heights
in which foam is born from two soaring bodies.

Oh, lucid marvel of your singing body
strewing kisses on your wakened skin:
sparkling dome of sky, filled with night's beauty,
that moistens my breast with stars or foams!

Lejos ya la agonía, la soledad gimiente,
las torpes aves bajas que gravemente rozaron mi frente en los oscuros
    días del dolor.

Lejos los mares ocultos que enviaban sus aguas,
pesadas, gruesas, lentas, bajo la extinguida zona de la luz.

Ahora vuelto a tu claridad no es difícil
reconocer a los pájaros matinales que pían,
ni percibir en las mejillas los impalpables velos de la Aurora,
como es posible sobre los suaves pliegues de la tierra
divisar el duro, vivo, generoso desnudo del día,
que hunde sus pies ligeros en unas aguas transparentes.

Dejadme entonces, vagas preocupaciones de ayer,
abandonar mis lentos trajes sin música,
como un árbol que depone su luto rumoroso,
su mate adiós a la tristeza,
para exhalar feliz sus hojas verdes, sus azules campánulas
y esa gozosa espuma que cabrillea en su copa
cuando por primera vez le invade la riente Primavera.

Después del amor, de la felicidad activa del amor, reposado,
tendido, imitando descuidadamente un arroyo,
yo reflejo las nubes, los pájaros, las futuras estrellas,
a tu lado, oh reciente, oh viva, oh entregada;
y me miro en tu cuerpo, en tu forma blanda, dulcísima, apagada,
como se contempla la tarde que colmadamente termina.

Far distant now the agony, the moaning loneliness,
the clumsy birds so low they gravely brushed my forehead on the
   somber days of pain.

Far off the hidden seas that sent their waters,
heavy, thick, and slow beneath the darkened zone of light.

Now that your radiance has come again, it is not hard
to recognize the morning birds that chirped,
nor to perceive upon their cheeks Aurora's insubstantial veils,
as one above the earth's soft gentle folds can sight
the hard, living full-fleshed naked figure of the day,
sinking her airy feet into transparent waters.

Allow me then, obscure preoccupations of another day,
to leave behind my heavy unmelodious garb
just as a tree may shed its rustling mourning clothes,
its lusterless farewell to sadness,
and exhale in its joy its verdant leaves, its bluebells,
and that joyous foam that shimmers in its cup
when laughing Springtime invades it for the first time.

After love, the active happiness of love, at rest,
stretched out, in unmindful imitation of a stream,
I reflect the clouds, the birds, the future stars,
there by your side, oh recent, live, submissive being;
and in your body I behold myself, and in your supple form, so
   tender, now extinguished,
as one contemplates the evening that ends in plenitude.

LOS DORMIDOS

¿Qué voz entre los pájaros de esta noche de ensueño
dulcemente modula los nombres en el aire?
¡Despertad! Una luna redonda gime o canta
entre velos, sin sombra, sin destino, invocándoos.
Un cielo herido a luces, a hachazos, llueve el oro
sin estrellas, con sangre, que en un torso resbala;
revelador envío de un destino llamando
a los dormidos siempre bajo los cielos vívidos.

¡Despertad! Es el mundo, es su música. ¡Oídla!
La tierra vuela alerta, embriagada de visos,
de deseos, desnuda, sin túnica, radiante,
bacante en los espacios que un seno muestra hermoso,
azulado de venas, de brillos, de turgencia.

¡Mirad! ¿No véis un muslo deslumbrador que avanza?
¿Un bulto victorioso, un ropaje estrellado
que retrasadamente revuela, cruje, azota
los siderales vientos azules, empapados?

¿No sentís en la noche un clamor? ¡Ah dormidos,
sordos sois a los cánticos! Dulces copas se alzan:
¡Oh estrellas mías, vino celeste, dadme toda
vuestra locura, dadme vuestros bordes lucientes!
Mis labios saben siempre sorberos, mi garganta

THE SLEEPERS

What voice among the birds this night of dreams
so gently modulates names in the air?
Awake! A full round moon moans or sings among
the veils, without destiny or shadow, invoking you.
A sky wounded by light and ax-blows rains a
starless golden shower, red as blood, that slides onto a torso;
the revealing message of a destiny that calls
to sleepers still beneath the vivid skies.

Awake! Here is the world, here is its music! Hear it play!
The earth soars vigilant, enraptured with its gleams,
its longings, naked, gownless, radiant,
a bacchante in the distance who bares her lovely breast,
blue with veins, with brightness and turgidity.

Look up! Do you not see a dazzling thigh advancing?
A triumphal mass, a garment set with stars
that slowly flutters, rustles, whips
the winds sidereal and blue, drenched with rain?

In the nighttime do you hear no shout? Ah sleepers,
are you so deaf to canticles! Sweet cups are raised:
Oh stars of mine, celestial wine, give me all
your madness, give me all your shining shores!
My lips know how to drink you in, my throat

se enciende de sapiencia, mis ojos brillan dulces.
Toda la noche en mí destellando, ilumina
vuestro sueño, oh dormidos, oh muertos, oh acabados.

Pero no; muertamente callados, como lunas
de piedra, en tierra, sordos permanecéis, sin tumba.
Una noche de velos, de plumas, de miradas,
vuela por los espacios llevándoos, insepultos.

ignites with wisdom, my eyes are softly shining.
All the night sparkling within me illuminates
your dream, oh sleepers, oh dead ones, forever ended.

But no; in deathly silence, like moons
of stone, in the ground, forever deaf you'll stay, without a tomb.
A night of veils, of plumage and of glances
soars through space and carries you away, unburied.

MUERTE EN EL PARAÍSO

¿Era acaso a mis ojos el clamor de la selva,
selva de amor resonando en los fuegos
del crepúsculo,
lo que a mí se dolía con su voz casi humana?

¡Ah, no! ¿Qué pecho desnudo, qué tibia carne casi celeste,
qué luz herida por la sangre emitía
su cristalino arrullo de una boca entreabierta,
trémula todavía de un gran beso intocado?

Un suave resplandor entre las ramas latía
como perdiendo luz, y sus dulces quejidos
tenuemente surtían de un pecho transparente.
¿Qué leve forma agotada, qué ardido calor humano
me dio su turbia confusión de colores
para mis ojos, en un póstumo resplandor intangible,
gema de luz perdiendo sus palabras de dicha?

Inclinado sobre aquel cuerpo desnudo,
sin osar adorar con mi boca su esencia,
cerré mis ojos deslumbrados por un ocaso de sangre,
de luz, de amor, de soledad, de fuego.

Rendidamente tenté su frente de mármol
coloreado, como un cielo extinguiéndose.
Apliqué mis dedos sobre sus ojos abatidos
y aún acerqué a su rostro mi boca, porque acaso
de unos labios brillantes aún otra luz bebiese.

DEATH IN PARADISE

Was what my eyes perceived perhaps the jungle's clamor,
love's jungle resounding in the fires
of twilight,
that so deeply pained me with its almost human voice?

Ah no! What naked breast, what tepid flesh almost celestial,
what light pierced through by blood sending forth
its crystal river from a half-open mouth,
tremulous still from a great unfelt kiss?

Among the branches a suave resplendence throbbed
like a dying light, and its sweet laments
flowed tenuously from a transparent breast.
What frail exhausted form, what intrepid human warmth
spread out before my eyes, with a posthumous
intangible resplendence, its turbid and profuse display of colors
like a jewel of light that sheds its words of happiness?

Inclining above that naked body,
not daring to adore its essence with my lips,
I closed my eyes, blinded by a blood-red sunset
of light, of love, of solitude, of fire.

Submissively I touched your brow of marble
with its colors of a sky reduced to embers.
I put my fingers on your downcast eyes
and even moved my lips close to your face, hoping
still to drink another light from other shining lips.

Sólo un sueño de vida sentí contra los labios
ya ponientes, un sueño de luz crepitante,
un amor que, aún caliente,
en mi boca abrasaba mi sed, sin darme vida.

Bebí, chupé, clamé. Un pecho exhausto,
quieto cofre de sol, desvariaba
interiormente sólo de resplandores dulces.
Y puesto mi pecho sobre el suyo, grité, llamé, deliré,
agité mi cuerpo, estrechando en mi seno sólo un cielo estrellado.

¡Oh dura noche fría! El cuerpo de mi amante,
tendido, parpadeaba, titilaba en mis brazos.
Avaramente contra mí ceñido todo,
sentí la gran bóveda oscura de su forma luciente,
y si besé su muerto azul, su esquivo amor,
sentí su cabeza estrellada sobre mi hombro aún fulgir
y darme su reciente, encendida soledad de la noche.

It was nothing but a dream of life I felt against those lips
already setting, a dream of crackling light,
a love still filled with warmth
that in my mouth parched my thirst but gave me no life.

I drank, I suckled, I cried out. A weary breast,
the sun's still coffer, was delirious within
from soft resplendences.
And with my breast against hers, I cried, I called, I raved,
I shook my body, holding tight within my breast only a star-filled sky.

Oh harsh cold night! The body of my lover,
lying there, was flickering and trembling in my arms.
With everything hungrily pressed against me,
I felt the great dark vaulting of her shining form,
and if I kissed her lifeless blue, her disdainful love,
I felt her starry head upon my shoulder shining still
and giving me her recent luminescent solitude of night.

MENSAJE

Amigos, no preguntéis a la gozosa mañana
por qué el sol intangible da su fuerza a los hombres.
Bebed su claro don, su lucidez en la sombra,
en los brazos amantes de ese azul inspirado,
y abrid los ojos sobre la belleza del mar, como del amor,
ebrios de luz sobre la hermosa vida,
mientras cantan los pájaros su mensaje infinito
y hay un presentimiento de espuma en vuestras frentes
y un rapto de deseo en los aires dichosos,
que como labios dulces trémulamente asedian.

Vosotros venís de la remota montaña,
quieta montaña de majestad velada,
pero no ignoráis la luz, porque en los ojos nace
cada mañana el mar con su azul intocable,
su inmarcesible brío luminoso y clamante,
palabra entera que un universo grita
mientras besa a la tierra con perdidas espumas.

Recogiendo del aire una voz, un deseo,
un misterio que una mano quizá asiera un día entre un vuelo de
    pájaros,
contempláis el amor, cósmico afán del hombre,
y esa fragante plenitud de la tierra
donde árboles colmados de primavera urgente
dan su luz o sus pomas a unos labios sedientos.

THE MESSAGE

Friends, do not ask the joyous morning
why the distant sun bestows its strength on men.
Drink its limpid gift, its brightness in the shadow,
in the loving arms of that inspired blue,
and open your eyes to the beauty of the sea, as though to love,
eyes drunk with light above life's loveliness,
while birds sing their infinite message
and on your brows a portent of foam appears,
and a rapture of desire in the auspicious winds
that like soft lips tremulously lay siege.

You came from the distant mountain,
a still mountain of veiled majesty,
but you are not unaware of the light, for in your eyes
the sea each morning with its matchless blue is born,
with its unfading bright demanding spirit,
a word in its entirety that a universe calls out
as it embraces earth with short-lived foams.

Gathering from the air a voice, a wish,
a mystery some hand one day may seize among a flight of birds,
you meditate on love, man's cosmic urge,
and that sweet fragrant plenitude of earth
where trees replete with urgent spring
give their light or apples to parched lips.

Mirad el vasto coro de las nubes,
alertas sobre el mar,
enardecidas reflejar el mensaje
de un sol de junio que abrasado convoca
a una sangre común con su luz despiadada.
Embebed en vuestra cabellera el rojo ardor de los besos inmensos
que se deshacen salpicados de brillos,
y destelle otra vez, y siempre, en vuestros ojos el verde piafador de
    las playas,
donde un galope oculto de mar rompe en espumas.
Besad la arena, acaso eco del sol, caliente a vino, a celeste mensaje,
licor de luz que en los labios chorrea
y trastorna en la ebria lucidez a las almas,
veladoras después en la noche de estrellas.

¡Ah! Amigos, arrojad lejos, sin mirar, los artefactos tristes,
tristes ropas, palabras, palos ciegos, metales,
y desnudos de majestad y pureza frente al grito del mundo,
lanzad el cuerpo al abismo de la mar, de la luz, de la dicha inviolada,
mientras el universo, ascua pura y final, se consume.

Look at the vast ensemble of clouds
on watch above the sea,
as ablaze they reflect the message
of a flaming June sun that convokes
a common blood with its heartless light.
Saturate your silken hair with the carmine ardor of gigantic kisses
that dissolve and fall in flashing gleams,
and let shine again, and forever, within your eyes the green hoofbeat
    of the shore
where the sea's secret gallop bursts into spray.
Kiss the sand, the sun's chance echo, hot with wine and a celestial
    message,
a liquored stream of light that gushes down on lips
and in its drunken clarity disturbs those souls
who keep their vigil in the starry night.

Ah, friends, cast far away, without a glance, those sorry artifacts,
weary clothing, words, unseeing staffs, the metals,
and stripped of majesty and purity before the strident shouting of the
    world,
hurl into the deep abyss of sea, of light, of happiness inviolate, your
    body,
as the universe, a pure and fatal ember, is consumed.

LA LLUVIA

La cintura no es rosa.
No es ave. No son plumas.
La cintura es la lluvia,
fragilidad, gemido
que a ti se entrega. Ciñe,
mortal, tú con tu brazo
un agua dulce, queja
de amor. Estrecha, estréchala.
Toda la lluvia un junco
parece. ¡Cómo ondula,
si hay viento, si hay tu brazo,
mortal que, hoy sí, la adoras!

RAIN

That slender waist is not a rose.
Is not a bird. Is not feathers.
That slender waistline is the rain,
a fragile thing, a moaning sound
that yields herself to you. Clasp,
mortal, with your arm
the soft, sweet water, a lament
of love. Embrace her, hold her tight.
All the rain appears to be
a slender reed. How she sways
if there is wind, if there is your arm,
mortal who, today, adores her!

EL SOL

Leve, ingrávida apenas,
la sandalia. Pisadas
sin carne. Diosa sola,
demanda a un mundo planta
para su cuerpo, arriba
solar. No cabellera
digáis; cabello ardiente.
Decid sandalia, leve
pisada; decid sólo,
no tierra, grama dulce
que cruje a ese destello
tan suave que la adora
cuando la pisa. ¡Oh, siente
tu luz, tu grave tacto
solar! Aquí, sintiéndote,
la tierra es cielo. Y brilla.

SUN

So light, almost afloat,
the sandal. Fleshless steps.
A goddess lone on high
asks earth to give feet
to her solar body.
Don't speak of flowing hair
nor of her burning tresses.
Speak of her sandal, of
her airy step; speak not
of earth, but tender grass
that rustles at her gleam,
so gentle it adores
her very step. Just feel
your solemn solar touch,
your light! Here, feeling you,
earth becomes heaven. And shines.

LA PALABRA

La palabra fue un día
calor: un labio humano.
Era la luz como mañana joven; más: relámpago
en esta eternidad desnuda. Amaba
alguien. Sin antes ni después. Y el verbo
brotó. ¡Palabra sola y pura
por siempre —Amor— en el espacio bello!

WORD

The word one day was
warmth: a human lip.
The light was like a dawning day; still more: a lightning flash
in an eternity stripped bare. It loved
someone. Without before or after. And the word
sprang forth. A single word and pure
forever—Love—in that resplendent space!

LA TIERRA

La tierra conmovida
exhala vegetal
su gozo. ¡Hela: ha nacido!
Verde rubor, hoy boga
por un espacio aún nuevo.
¡Qué encierra? Sola, pura
de sí, nadie la habita.
Sólo la gracia muda,
primigenia, del mundo,
va en astros, leve, virgen,
entre la luz dorada.

EARTH

The earth with fervent zeal
exhales its vegetal
exuberance. Behold:
it has been born! Green blush,
today it sails through space
still new. What does it hold?
Purely itself, no one
yet inhabits it. The
world's mute virgin grace,
primordial, moves through stars
across the golden light.

EL FUEGO

Todo el fuego suspende
la pasión. ¡Luz es sola!
Mirad cuán puro se alza
hasta lamer los cielos,
mientras las aves todas
por él vuelan. ¡No abrasa!
¿Y el hombre? Nunca. Libre
todavía de ti,
humano, está ese fuego.
Luz es, luz inocente.
¡Humano: nunca nazcas!

FIRE

All fire brings passion's end.
Light is solitary!
See how pure it rises
till it licks the skies,
while cross it birds all
pass in flight. It does not burn!
And man? No, never. Free
of you, still,
human being, is fire.
It is light, innocent light.
Human: never come to life!

EL AIRE

Aún más que el mar, el aire,
más inmenso que el mar, está tranquilo.
Alto velar de lucidez sin nadie.
Acaso la corteza pudo un día,
de la tierra, sentirte, humano. Invicto,
el aire ignora que habitó en tu pecho.
Sin memoria, inmortal, el aire esplende.

AIR

More so than the sea, the air,
far vaster than the sea, is tranquil.
High solitary vigil of lucidity.
Perhaps one day the earth's crust
could feel you, humankind. Unvanquished,
air forgets it once lived inside your breast.
Immortal, lacking memory, radiant air.

EL MAR

¿Quién dijo acaso que la mar suspira,
labio de amor hacia las playas, triste?
Dejad que envuelta por la luz campee.
¡Gloria, gloria en la altura, y en la mar, el oro!
¡Ah soberana luz que envuelve, canta
la inmarcesible edad del mar gozante!
Allá, reverberando,
sin tiempo, el mar existe.
¡Un corazón de dios sin muerte, late!

SEA

Who would have said the sea sighs sadly
like a lip of love directed toward the shore?
Allow it swathed in light to wander as it will.
Glory, glory in the skies, and gold upon the sea!
Ah sovereign swaddling light, exalt
in song the joyous sea's undying age!
Reverberating there,
outside time, the sea exists.
Heart of a deathless god, throb on!

5

A UNA MUCHACHA DESNUDA

Cuán delicada muchacha,
tú que me miras con tus ojos oscuros.
Desde el borde de ese río, con las ondas por medio,
veo tu dibujo preciso sobre un verde armonioso.
No es el desnudo como llama que agostara la hierba,
o como brasa súbita que cenizas presagia,
sino que quieta, derramada, fresquísima,
eres tú primavera matinal que en un soplo llegase.

Imagen fresca de la primavera que blandamente se posa.
Un lecho de césped virgen recogido ha tu cuerpo,
cuyos bordes descansan como un río aplacado.
Tendida estás, preciosa, y tu desnudo canta
suavemente oreado por las brisas de un valle.
Ah, musical muchacha que graciosamente ofrecida
te rehusas, allá en la orilla remota.
Median las ondas raudas que de ti me separan,
eterno deseo dulce, cuerpo, nudo de dicha,
que en la hierba reposas como un astro celeste.

TO A NAKED GIRL

What a fragile figure of a girl,
you who look at me with great dark eyes.
From upon that river's bank, kept by waves apart,
I see your shape precisely sketched against a harmony of green.
It is not a flamelike nude who sets the grass ablaze
or like a sudden ember foreboding future ash,
—but you, still, overflowing, fresh,
a dawning spring who arrived upon a gust of wind.

Fresh image of the springtime that gently now alights.
A bed of virgin lawn has gathered up your body,
whose contours like a placid river take their rest.
You lie there, lovely beauty, and your nude figure sings
gently cooled by breezes from a valley.
Ah, girl of many melodies, graciously you offered
then withdrew yourself, there on the distant shore.
Between us rushing waves keep me from your side,
eternal sweet desire, embodiment of happiness,
that like a celestial body reposes on the grass.

DESTERRADO DE TU CUERPO

Ligera, graciosamente leve, aún me sonríes. ¿Besas?
De ti despierto, amada, de tus brazos me alzo
y veo como un río que en soledad se canta.
Hermoso cuerpo extenso, ¿me he mirado sólo en tus ondas,
o ha sido sangre mía la que en tus ondas llevas?

Pero de ti me alzo. De ti surto. ¿Era un nudo
de amor? ¿Era un silencio poseso? No lo sabremos nunca.
Mutilación me llamo. No tengo nombre; sólo
memoria soy quebrada de ti misma. Oh mi patria,
oh cuerpo de donde vivo desterrado,
oh tierra mía,
reclámame.
Súmame yo en tu seno feraz. Completo viva,
con un nombre, una sangre, que nuestra unión se llame.

EXILED FROM YOUR BODY

Weightless, pleasingly slight, you still smile at me. Do you kiss?
I awaken from you, loved one, from your arms I rise
and see you like a river singing its song in solitude.
Long slender body, did I see only myself in your waves,
or was it my blood that in your waves you carry?

But I arise from you. From you I spurt. Was it a bond
of love? Was it a spirit-haunted silence? We shall never know.
Mutilation I am called. I have no name; for I am
only memory severed from you. Oh my homeland,
oh body from which exiled now I live,
oh earth of mine,
reclaim me.
Let me drown in your fertile breast. Entirely alive,
with a name, a blood, that invokes our union.

EL PIE EN LA ARENA

El pie desnudo. Sólo
su huella; sólo el leve
trasunto. Aquí el perfume
estuvo. ¡Quién pudiera
seguirte, aire que un día
arrebataste la última
sospecha de una carne!
Huella desnuda, intacta.
Plinto de mi deseo,
donde hoy se yergue entera
la irrenunciable estatua.

FOOTPRINT IN THE SAND

A shoeless foot. Nothing
but its print remains; only
the fragile likeness. Here
there was a scent. Who could
pursue you, air that one day
carried off the ultimate
suspicion of man's flesh!
Untouched, a naked footprint.
The threshold of my longing
where today there stands entire
the irrefutable statue.

NOCHE CERRADA

Ah triste, ah inmensamente triste
que en la noche oscurísima buscas ojos oscuros,
ve sólo el terciopelo de la sombra
donde resbalan leves las silenciosas aves.
Apenas si una pluma espectral rozará tu frente,
como un presagio del vacío inmediato.

Inmensamente triste tú miras la impenetrable sombra en que respiras.
Álzala con tu pecho penoso; un oleaje
de negror invencible, como columna altísima
gravita en el esclavo corazón oprimido.
Ah, cuán hermosas allá arriba en los cielos
sobre la columnaria noche arden las luces,
los libertados luceros que ligeros circulan,
mientras tú los sostienes con tu pequeño pecho,
donde un árbol de piedra nocturna te somete.

NIGHT OF DARK CLOUDS

How sad, immensely sad
that in darkest night you search for dark eyes,
and only the shadow's velvet sees
the silent birds wheel high in weightless flight.
A spectral feather might scarcely graze your brow,
like an omen of impending emptiness.

Immeasurably sad, you gaze at the impenetrable shadow in which
    you breathe.
Raise it with your painful chest; a surging tide
of invincible blackness, like a towering column,
weighs on your enslaved, oppressed heart.
Oh, how beautiful above the columned night
the lights high in the heavens flame,
the unfettered stars circle swiftly,
while you sustain them with your little breast,
wherein a tree of night-black stone overpowers you.

CUERPO DE AMOR

Volcado sobre ti,
volcado sobre tu imagen derramada bajo los altos álamos inocentes,
tu desnudez se ofrece como un río escapando,
espuma dulce de tu cuerpo crujiente,
frío y fuego de amor que en mis brazos salpica.

Por eso, si acerco mi boca a tu corriente prodigiosa,
si miro tu azul soledad, donde un cielo aún me teme,
veo una nube que arrebata mis besos
y huye y clama mi nombre, y en mis brazos se esfuma.

Por eso, si beso tu pecho solitario,
si al poner mis labios tristísimos sobre tu piel incendiada
siento en la mejilla el labio dulce del poniente apagándose,
oigo una voz que gime, un corazón brillando,
un bulto hermoso que en mi boca palpita,
seno de amor, rotunda morbidez de la tarde.

Sobre tu piel palabras o besos cubren, ciegan,
apagan su rosado resplandor erguidísimo,
y allí mis labios oscuros celan, hacen, dan noche,
avaramente ardientes: ¡pecho hermoso de estrellas!

Tu vientre níveo no teme el frío de esos primeros vientos,
helados, duros como manos ingratas,
que rozan y estremecen esa tibia magnolia,
pálida luz que en la noche fulgura.

LOVE'S BODY

Overturned above you,
overturned above your image spilled beneath the tall chaste poplars,
your nudity offers itself like a river overflowing,
the soft sweet spray of your rippling body,
cold and fire of love that spatters on my arms.

So, if now I move my lips near your prodigious current,
if I look at your azure solitude, where the sky is fearful of me still,
I see a cloud carry off my kisses,
and flee and shout my name, and vanish in my arms.

So, if now I kiss your lonely breast,
if I place my sad, sad lips upon your blazing flesh,
on my cheek I feel the gentle lip of the setting sun,
and I hear a moaning voice, a gleaming heart,
a comely figure throbbing in my mouth,
love's breast, well-rounded softness of the afternoon.

Upon your flesh, words or kisses shroud and blind,
extinguishing its rosy-tinted swollen splendor,
and my lightless lips mount vigil, grow and turn to night,
avaricious in their ardor: oh bosom beautiful with stars!

Your snow-white pelvis does not fear the cold of those first winds,
frozen, as harsh as thankless hands
that brush with chilling touch that warm magnolia,
the pallid light glowing in the night.

Déjame así, sobre tu cuerpo libre,
bajo la luz castísima de la luna intocada,
aposentar los rayos de otra luz que te besa,
boca de amor que crepita en las sombras
y recorre tu virgen revelación de espuma.

Apenas río, apenas labio, apenas seda azul eres tú, margen dulce,
que te entregas riendo, amarilla en la noche,
mientras mi sombra finge el claroscuro de plata
de unas hojas felices que en la brisa cantasen.

Abierta, penetrada de la noche, el silencio
de la tierra eres tú: ¡oh mía, como un mundo en los brazos!
No pronuncies mi nombre: brilla sólo en lo oscuro.
Y ámame, poseída de mí, cuerpo a cuerpo en la dicha,
beso puro que estela deja eterna en los aires.

Let me be here, on your unbridled body,
beneath the chaste pure light of the still-untouched moon,
sheltering the rays of other light that kisses you,
a mouth of love that crackles in the shadows
and journeys across your virgin foaming revelation.

Barely river, barely lip, barely sky-blue silk you are, soft border
that surrenders laughingly, yellow in the night,
while my shadow imitates the light and shuttered silver
of a joyous foliage that in a breeze would sing.

Open, penetrated by the night, the silence
of the earth is you: oh mine, like a world here in my arms!
Do not pronounce my name: just shine there in the dark.
And love me, possessed by me, body next to body in our happiness,
pure kiss that leaves its wake forever in the upper air.

CABELLERA NEGRA

¿Por qué te miro, con tus ojos oscuros,
terciopelo viviente en que mi vida lastimo?
Cabello negro, luto donde entierro mi boca,
oleaje doloroso donde mueren mis besos,
orilla en fin donde mi voz al cabo se extingue y moja
tu majestad, oh cabellera que en una almohada derramada reinas.

En tu borde se rompen,
como en una playa oscura, mis deseos continuos.
¡Oh inundada: aún existes, sobrevives, imperas!
Toda tú victoriosa como un pico en los mares.

BLACK TRESSES

Why do I look at you, with your eyes so dark,
a living velvet in which I wound my life?
Black tresses, mourning in which I inter my mouth,
the painful surge of tide wherein my kisses die,
the shore on which my voice at last falls silent and floods
your majesty, oh sovereign hair outspread upon a pillow.

Against your shore,
as on a darkened beach, my never-ending longings break.
Oh flooded beauty: you exist, survive, prevail!
All of you, victorious, like a pinnacle in the sea.

CUERPO SIN AMOR

Pero no son tus ojos, tranquilos;
pero no serán nunca tus ojos los que yo ame.
Derribada, soberbia, centrada por el fuego nocturno de tus pupilas,
tú me contemplas, quieto río que un astro lunar frío devuelves.
Toda la noche hermosa sobre tu cuerpo brilla
y tú la escupes, oh superficie que un resplandor gélido otorgas.
La noche se desliza sobre tu forma. (¡Ah frío del mundo,
quién mirará tu quieto, tu sideral transcurso sobre un cuerpo
   estrellado!)
No améis esa presencia que entre los verdes quietos oscuramente
   pasa.
Cuerpo o río que helado hacia la mar se escurre,
donde nunca el humano beberá con su boca,
aunque un ojo caliente de su hermosura sufra.

LOVELESS BODY

But they are not your eyes, those tranquil ones;
but they will never be the eyes I love.
Cast down to earth, superbly proud, centered by your pupils'
    nocturnal fire,
you contemplate me, quiet river that reflects a dim cold lunar star.
All the beauty of the night shines down upon your body
and you spit it back, oh surface that bestows a frozen splendor.
Night glides down upon your form. (Ah coldness of the world,
who will behold your still, sidereal passage across a star-emblazoned
    body!)
Do not love that presence that passes darkly through the quiet greens.
Body or river flowing frozen toward the sea
from which no human mouth will drink,
even should an eye warmed by your beauty suffer.

EL PERFUME

Chupar tu vida sobre tus labios,
no es quererte en la muerte.
Chupar tu vida, amante,
para que lenta mueras
de mí, de mí que mato.
Para agotar tu vida
como una rosa exhausta.
Color, olor: mis venas
saben a ti: allí te abres.
Ebriamente encendido,
tú me recorres. Toda,
toda mi sangre es sólo
perfume. Tú me habitas,
aroma arrebatado
que por mí te despliegas,
que como sangre corres
por mí: ¡que a mí me pueblas!

THE PERFUME

To suck your life upon your lips
does not mean loving you in death.
to suck your very life, my love,
so that you slowly die
of me, your murderer.
So I deplete life
like a withered rose.
Color, odor: my very veins
taste of you: there you unfold.
Drunkenly inflamed, across me
now you make your journeys. All,
all of my blood becomes only
perfume. You inhabit me,
heady enrapturing aroma
that in my body grows and spreads,
that like blood goes pulsing
through me: for you people me!

6

PADRE MÍO

A mi hermana.

Lejos estás, padre mío, allá en tu reino de las sombras.
Mira a tu hijo, oscuro en esta tiniebla huérfana,
lejos de la benévola luz de tus ojos continuos.
Allí nací, crecí; de aquella luz pura
tomé vida, y aquel fulgor sereno
se embebió en esta forma, que todavía despide,
como un eco apagado, tu luz resplandeciente.

Bajo la frente poderosa, mundo entero de vida,
mente completa que un humano alcanzara,
sentí la sombra que protegió mi infancia. Leve, leve,
resbaló así la niñez como alígero pie sobre una hierba noble,
y si besé a los pájaros, si pude posar mis labios
sobre tantas alas fugaces que una aurora empujara,
fue por ti, por tus benévolos ojos que presidieron mi nacimiento
y fueron como brazos que por encima de mi testa cernían
la luz, la luz tranquila, no heridora a mis ojos de niño.

Alto, padre, como una montaña que pudiera inclinarse,
que pudiera vencerse sobre mi propia frente descuidada
y besarme tan luminosamente, tan silenciosa y puramente
como la luz que pasa por las crestas radiantes
donde reina el azul de los cielos purísimos.

Por tu pecho bajaba una cascada luminosa de bondad, que tocaba
luego mi rostro y bañaba mi cuerpo aún infantil, que emergía

FATHER MINE

To my sister.

In your shadowy kingdom, you are far away, father mine.
Look down upon your son, an orphan in this darkness lost,
far from the loving light that shone unceasing in your eyes.
There I was born, there grew; from that pure light
I took my life, and all that quiet splendor
was absorbed into this form that like a faded echo
radiates your still resplendent light.

Beneath your mighty brow, a world replete with life,
a mind as full as any man could claim,
I found the sheltered haven of my youth. With simple ease
my childhood years slipped by, like nimble feet on a stately lawn,
and if I kissed those birds, if I could place my lips
upon those many soaring wings that dawn had set astir,
it was for you, for your loving eyes that presided over my birth
and, like arms above my head, screened out
the light, the tranquil light, lest it wound my infant eyes.

Tall, my father, like a mountain that could bend
down to my carefree brow
and kiss me with a luminosity as pure and silent
as the light that shimmers on the radiant crests
where the blue of purest skies is sovereign.

Through your breast flowed a lustrous flood of love that touched
my face and bathed my infant body; from your quiet strength

de tu fuerza tranquila como desnudo, reciente,
nacido cada día de ti, porque tú fuiste padre
diario, y cada día yo nací de tu pecho, exhalado
de tu amor, como acaso mensaje de tu seno purísimo.
Porque yo nací entero cada día, entero y tierno siempre,
y débil y gozoso cada día hollé naciendo
la hierba misma intacta: pisé leve, estrené brisas,
henchí también mi seno, y miré el mundo
y lo vi bueno. Bueno tú, padre mío, mundo mío, tú sólo.

Hasta la orilla del mar condujiste mi mano.
Benévolo y potente tú como un bosque en la orilla,
yo sentí mis espaldas guardadas contra el viento estrellado.
Pude sumergir mi cuerpo reciente cada aurora en la espuma,
y besar a la mar candorosa en el día,
siempre olvidada, siempre, de su noche de lutos.

Padre, tú me besaste con labios de azul sereno.
Limpios de nubes veía yo tus ojos,
aunque a veces un velo de tristeza eclipsaba a mi frente
esa luz que sin duda de los cielos tomabas.
Oh padre altísimo, oh tierno padre gigantesco
que así, en los brazos, desvalido, me hubiste.

Huérfano de ti, menudo como entonces, caído sobre una hierba
     triste,
heme hoy aquí, padre, sobre el mundo en tu ausencia,

I emerged newborn, naked each day, for each day you
fathered me, and I each day from your chest was born,
exhaled by your love, like a message from your purest breast.
Because each day I was reborn entire, a whole and new-made being,
weak yet joyous, each day I found the grass
luxuriate anew; I walked there with a gentle step, first felt the breeze,
filled my lungs with air, and looked upon the world
and found it good. You, father mine, were good, my very world,
    and you alone.

To the ocean's shore you led my hand.
With you benevolent and strong like a forest on the shore,
I felt my shoulders sheltered from the star-chilled wind.
Each breaking day I bathed my newborn body in the foam,
and kissed the sea whose silver whiteness every day
always forgot, always, its nighttime mourning.

Father, you kissed me with lips of peaceful blue.
I saw your unbeclouded eyes,
though at times a veil of sadness eclipsed from my view
the light you doubtlessly acquired from heaven.
Almighty father, giant tender father,
you who took me, helpless, in your arms.

Orphaned by you, as small as I was then, fallen on the sullen grass,
Here I am today, father, in a world that you have left,

mientras pienso en tu forma sagrada, habitadora acaso de una sombra
  amorosa,
por la que nunca, nunca tu corazón me olvida.

Oh padre mío, seguro estoy que en la tiniebla fuerte
tú vives y me amas. Que un vigor poderoso,
un latir, aún revienta en la tierra.
Y que unas ondas de pronto, desde un fondo, sacuden
a la tierra y la ondulan, y a mis pies se estremece.

Pero yo soy de carne todavía. Y mi vida
es de carne, padre, padre mío. Y aquí estoy,
solo, sobre la tierra quieta, menudo como entonces, sin verte,
derribado sobre los inmensos brazos que horriblemente te imitan.

while I contemplate your sacred form some loving shadow may
    inhabit still,
through which never, never will your heart forget me.

Oh father mine, I know that in that solid dark
you live and love me. That a mighty force,
a throbbing, still bursts within the earth.
And that sudden great waves come from the depths to shake
the earth and make it sway, and at my feet it trembles.

But I am still of flesh. And my life
is of flesh, father, father mine. And here I am
alone upon the quiet earth, as small as I was then, not seeing you,
prostrate now upon the enormous arms that ghoulishly pretend to be
    you.

AL HOMBRE

¿Por qué protestas, hijo de la luz,
humano que transitorio en la tierra,
redimes por un instante tu materia sin vida?
¿De dónde vienes, mortal que del barro has llegado
para un momento brillar y regresar después a tu apagada patria?
Si un soplo, arcilla finita, erige tu vacilante forma
y calidad de dios tomas en préstamo,
no, no desafíes cara a cara a ese sol poderoso que fulge
y compasivo te presta cabellera de fuego.
Por un soplo celeste redimido un instante,
alzas tu incandescencia temporal a los seres.
Hete aquí luminoso, juvenil, perennal a los aires.
Tu planta pisa el barro de que ya eres distinto.
¡Oh, cuán engañoso, hermoso humano que con testa de oro
el sol piadoso coronado ha tu frente!
¡Cuán soberbia tu masa corporal, diferente sobre la tierra madre,
que cual perla te brinda!
Mas mira, mira que hoy, ahora mismo, el sol declina tristemente en
    los montes.
Míralo rematar ya de pálidas luces,
de tristes besos cenizosos de ocaso
tu frente oscura. Mira tu cuerpo extinto cómo acaba en la noche.
Regresa tú, mortal, humilde, pura arcilla apagada,
a tu certera patria que tu pie sometía.
He aquí la inmensa madre que de ti no es distinta.
Y, barro tú en el barro, totalmente perdura.

TO MAN

Why do you protest, child of the light,
transient creature on the earth,
redeeming for an instant your lifeless matter?
Where are you from, mortal who from dust has come
to shine here for a moment, then return to your darkened homeland?
If a breath, a finite clay, inflates your indecisive form
and you take on characteristics of the gods,
no, do not challenge face to face that powerful refulgent sun
that mercifully shares its mane of fire.
By a breath redeemed for one brief instant
you lift your short-lived incandescence toward all beings.
Here you are luminous, youthful, perennial in the air.
Your foot treads the clay that formed you.
How deceitful, handsome mortal—with head of gold
the clement sun has crowned your brow!
How matchless is your body's mass, so distinctive from the mother
    earth
that like a proffered pearl sustains you!
But look, look how sadly at this very moment of the day the sun
    declines into the mountains.
Look how it marks for death
with paling lights, with the sunset's ashen kisses
your darkened brow. Look how your extinct body comes to nothing
    in the night.
Return then, mortal, humble, pure lifeless clay,
to your certain homeland that your feet have conquered.
Here lies the boundless mother indistinct from you.
And you, dust within the dust, persist in your entirety.

ADIÓS A LOS CAMPOS

No he de volver, amados cerros, elevadas montañas,
gráciles ríos fugitivos que sin adiós os vais.
Desde esta suma de piedra temerosa diviso el valle.
Lejos el sol poniente, hermoso y robusto todavía, colma de amarillo
  esplendor
la cañada tranquila.
Y allá remota la llanura dorada donde verdea siempre el inmarchito
  día,
muestra su plenitud sin fatiga bajo un cielo completo.
¡Todo es hermoso y grande! El mundo está sin límites.
Y sólo mi ojo humano adivina allá lejos la linde, fugitiva
mas terca en sus espumas,
de un mar de día espléndido que de un fondo de nácares tornasolado
  irrumpe.

Erguido en esta cima, montañas repetidas, yo os contemplo, sangre
  de mi vivir que amasó vuestra piedra.
No soy distinto, y os amo. Inútilmente esas plumas de los ligeros
  vientos pertinaces,
alas de cóndor o, en lo bajo,
diminutas alillas de graciosos jilgueros,
brillan al sol con suavidad: la piedra
por mí tranquila os habla, mariposas sin duelo.
Por mí la hierba tiembla hacia la altura, más celeste que el ave.
Y todo ese gemido de la tierra, ese grito que siento

FAREWELL TO THE FIELDS

I must not return, beloved hills, high mountains,
fleet graceful rivers that depart without farewell.
From this fearsome aggregate of stone I perceive the valley.
Far off, the setting sun, still beautiful and strong, fills with yellow
   splendor
the tranquil glen.
And on the distant golden plain the unblighted day always turns to
   green,
displays its vibrant plenitude beneath a perfect sky.
All is beautiful and grand! The world is without boundary.
And my human eye alone discerns there the distant border, fugitive
but stubborn in its foam,
of a sea of splendid day that from a depth of iridescent pearly grays
   erupts.

Standing high upon this summit, I look upon you, boundless peaks,
   blood of my living that amassed your stone.
I am no different from you, and I love you. In vain those feathers of
   the light persistent winds,
a condor's wings, or far below,
the tiny winglets of the graceful linnets
shine with softness in the sun: the stone
speaks quietly through me to you, butterflies with no sorrows.
Through me the grasses tremble toward the heights, more celestial
   than a bird.
And all this lamentation of the earth, this cry that I feel

propagándose loco de su raíz al fuego
de mi cuerpo, ilumina los aires,
no con palabras: vida, vida, llama, tortura,
o gloria soberana que sin saberlo escupo.

Aquí en esta montaña, quieto como la nube,
como la torva nube que aborrasca mi frente,
o dulce como el pájaro que en mi pupila escapa,
miro el inmenso día que inmensamente cede.
Oigo un rumor de foscas tempestades remotas
y penetro y distingo el vuelo tenue, en truenos,
de unas alas de polvo transparente que brillan.

Para mis labios quiero la piel terrible y dura
de ti, encina tremenda que solitaria abarcas
un firmamento verde de resonantes hojas.
Y aquí en mi boca quiero, pido amor, leve seda
de ti, rosa inviolada que como luz transcurres.

Sobre esta cima solitaria os miro,
campos que nunca volveréis por mis ojos.
Piedra de sol inmensa: entero mundo,
y el ruiseñor tan débil que en su borde lo hechiza.

spreading madly from its roots into the fire
of my body, illuminates the air,
not with words: with life, life, flame, torment,
or the sovereign glory I spit out unknowingly.

Here upon this mountain, tranquil like the cloud,
like the ferocious cloud that storms my brow,
or gentle like the bird that flits across my eye,
I behold the vast day that in its vastness now submits.
I hear the sound of sullen distant tempests
and I pierce and discern amid the thunderclaps
the tenuous flight and glimmer of wings of iridescent dust.

For my lips I want the terrible and solid flesh
of you, imposing oak, who in solitude embrace
a greening firmament of reverberating leaves.
And here inside my mouth I want, I ask for love, the fragile silk
of you, inviolate rose that like the light soon fades away.

Upon this solitary summit I behold you,
fields that never more will pass before my eyes.
Stone of boundless sun: a world entire,
and at its rim the frailest nightingale bewitches it.

DESTINO DE LA CARNE

No, no es eso. No miro
del otro lado del horizonte un cielo.
No contemplo unos ojos tranquilos, poderosos,
que aquietan a las aguas feroces que aquí braman.
No miro esa cascada de luces que descienden
de una boca hasta un pecho, hasta unas manos blandas,
finitas, que a este mundo contienen, atesoran.

Por todas partes veo cuerpos desnudos, fieles
al cansancio del mundo. Carne fugaz que acaso
nació para ser chispa de luz, para abrasarse
de amor y ser la nada sin memoria, la hermosa
redondez de la luz.
Y que aquí está, aquí está, marchitamente eterna,
sucesiva, constante, siempre, siempre cansada.

Es inútil que un viento remoto, con forma vegetal, o una lengua,
lama despacio y largo su volumen, lo afile,
lo pula, lo acaricie, lo exalte.
Cuerpos humanos, rocas cansadas, grises bultos
que a la orilla del mar conciencia siempre
tenéis de que la vida no acaba, no, heredándose.
Cuerpos que mañana repetidos, infinitos, rodáis
como una espuma lenta, desengañada, siempre.
¡Siempre carne del hombre, sin luz! Siempre rodados

FLESH'S DESTINY

No, it's not that at all. On the
horizon's other side, I do not see a sky.
I do not perceive the tranquil potent eyes
that calm the savage waters roaring here.
I do not see that waterfall of lights that cascade
from a mouth to a breast, to soft and
finite hands that contain this world and treasure it.

Everywhere I see nude bodies, faithful
to the world's fatigue. Short-lived flesh that perhaps
was born to be a spark of light, to consume itself
in love and be a nothing without memory, the lovely
roundness of the light.
And here it is, here it is, fadedly eternal,
successive, constant, ever and forever tired.

It is useless for a distant wind, of leafy form, or a tongue
to lick slowly and at length its mass, to taper it,
to polish it, caress it, and to worship it.
Human bodies, weary rocks, gray hulks
on the seashore, you are ever conscious
that life does not end, no, but relives its legacy.
Bodies infinite and repeated, tomorrow and forever
you exist like a languid disillusioned wave.
Always human flesh, devoid of light! Always rolling

desde allá, de un océano sin origen que envía
ondas, ondas, espumas, cuerpos cansados, bordes
de un mar que no se acaba y que siempre jadea en sus orillas.

Todos, multiplicados, repetidos, sucesivos, amontonáis la carne,
la vida, sin esperanza, monótonamente iguales bajo los cielos hoscos
    que impasibles se heredan.
Sobre ese mar de cuerpos que aquí vierten sin tregua, que aquí
    rompen
redondamente y quedan mortales en las playas,
no se ve, no, ese rápido esquife, ágil velero
que con quilla de acero rasgue, sesgue,
abra sangre de luz y raudo escape
hacia el hondo horizonte, hacia el origen
último de la vida, al confín del océano eterno
que humanos desparrama
sus grises cuerpos. Hacia la luz, hacia esa escala ascendente de brillos
que de un pecho benigno hacia una boca sube,
hacia unos ojos grandes, totales que contemplan,
hacia unas manos mudas, finitas, que aprisionan,
donde cansados siempre, vitales, aún nacemos.

forth from there, a sourceless ocean sending
wave on wave, spume, weary bodies, borders
of a sea that never ends and lies forever gasping on its shores.

All of you, in multiplicity, recurring and successive, heap flesh on
    flesh,
life without hope, monotonously the same beneath sullen skies
    passively repeated.
Above this sea of bodies that unceasingly pour forth and break here
in circles and then lie dying on the beach,
no one sees, no, that rapid skiff, an agile vessel
whose keel of sharpened steel rips, cuts across,
frees the gleaming blood, and swiftly flees
toward the deep horizon, toward the final
origin of life at the confines of the eternal sea
that spills forth its
gray human bodies. Toward the light, toward that rising stair of
    brilliances
that from a loving breast ascends toward a mouth,
toward large full eyes that contemplate,
toward mute finite hands that subjugate,
where, weary still but ever vital, yet we are born.

CIUDAD DEL PARAÍSO

A mi ciudad de Málaga.

Siempre te ven mis ojos, ciudad de mis días marinos.
Colgada del imponente monte, apenas detenida
en tu vertical caída a las ondas azules,
pareces reinar bajo el cielo, sobre las aguas,
intermedia en los aires, como si una mano dichosa
te hubiera retenido, un momento de gloria, antes de hundirte para
    siempre en las olas amantes.

Pero tú duras, nunca desciendes, y el mar suspira
o brama, por ti, ciudad de mis días alegres,
ciudad madre y blanquísima donde viví, y recuerdo,
angélica ciudad que, más alta que el mar, presides sus espumas.

Calles apenas, leves, musicales. Jardines
donde flores tropicales elevan sus juveniles palmas gruesas.
Palmas de luz que sobre las cabezas, aladas,
mecen el brillo de la brisa y suspenden
por un instante labios celestiales que cruzan
con destino a las islas remotísimas, mágicas,
que allá en el azul índigo, libertadas, navegan.

Allí también viví, allí, ciudad graciosa, ciudad honda.
Allí, donde los jóvenes resbalan sobre la piedra amable,
y donde las rutilantes paredes besan siempre
a quienes siempre cruzan, hervidores, en brillos.

CITY OF PARADISE

To my city of Málaga.

My eyes always see you, city of my days beside the sea.
Hanging from the towering mountain's side and scarcely
in your headlong plunge toward the sea detained,
you seem to reign beneath the sky, over the waters,
half suspended in the air, as if a providential hand
had held you back, a moment of glory, before it cast you for all time
    into the loving waves.

But you endure, never descending, and the sea sighs
or roars out for you, city of my happy days,
the mother city of a purest white in which I lived, and now recall,
angelic city high above the sea, overlooking its foamy surf.

Your streets are hardly streets, so light and musical. Gardens
in which flowers of the tropics raise their thick and youthful palms.
Palms of light that above their heads, like wings,
rock the cradled brilliance of the breeze and for a moment
hold suspended those celestial lips that pass above,
their destiny the far-off magic isles
that in the distant indigo of blue sail free.

There I too lived, there, gracious city, heartfelt city.
There, where the children play at sliding on the friendly stone,
and sparkling walls forever kiss
the people forever swarming there in splendor.

Allí fui conducido por una mano materna.
Acaso de una reja florida una guitarra triste
cantaba la súbita canción suspendida en el tiempo;
quieta la noche, más quieto el amante,
bajo la luna eterna que instantánea transcurre.

Un soplo de eternidad pudo destruirte,
ciudad prodigiosa, momento que en la mente de un Dios emergiste.
Los hombres por un sueño vivieron, no vivieron,
eternamente fúlgidos como un soplo divino.

Jardines, flores. Mar alentando como un brazo que anhela
a la ciudad voladora entre monte y abismo,
blanca en los aires, con calidad de pájaro suspenso
que nunca arriba. ¡Oh ciudad no en la tierra!

Por aquella mano materna fui llevado ligero
por tus calles ingrávidas. Pie desnudo en el día.
Pie desnudo en la noche. Luna grande. Sol puro.
Allí el cielo eras tú, ciudad que en él morabas.
Ciudad que en él volabas con tus alas abiertas.

There I was guided by a mother's hand.
By chance beside a flowered window's grille a sad guitar
would sound its sudden burst of song in time suspended;
then silent was the night, more silent still the lover,
underneath the timeless moon that in an instant passes by.

A breath of eternity could have destroyed you,
prodigious city, moment in which you emerged from a God's mind.
By a dream men lived there, did not live,
eternally as dazzling as an empyrean breath of wind.

Gardens, flowers. A sea extended like an arm that yearns
for the city soaring between high mountains and abyss,
white in the air, a bird stopped in flight
that never comes to land. Oh city not upon this earth!

By that maternal hand so gently I was taken
through your weightless streets. Barefoot in the daytime.
Barefoot in the night. Full moon. Pure sun.
You were the very sky, the city where you also dwelled.
The city where you soared with wings outspread.

HIJOS DE LOS CAMPOS

Vosotros los que consumís vuestras horas
en el trabajo gozoso y amor tranquilo pedís al mundo,
día a día gastáis vuestras fuerzas, y la noche benévola
os vela nutricia, y en el alba otra vez brotáis enteros.

Verdes fértiles. Hijos vuestros, menudas sombras humanas: cadenas
que desde vuestra limitada existencia arrojáis
—acaso puros y desnudos en el borde de un monte invisible— al
    mañana.
¡Oh ignorantes, sabios del vivir, que como hijos del sol pobláis el día!

Musculares, vegetales, pesados como el roble, tenaces como el arado
    que vuestra mano conduce,
arañáis a la tierra, no cruel, amorosa, que allí en su delicada piel os
    sustenta.
Y en vuestra frente tenéis la huella intensa y cruda del beso diario
del sol, que día a día os madura, hasta haceros oscuros y dulces
como la tierra misma, en la que, ya colmados, una noche, uniforme
    vuestro cuerpo tendéis.

Yo os veo como la verdad más profunda,
modestos y únicos habitantes del mundo,
última expresión de la noble corteza,
por la que todavía la tierra puede hablar con palabras.

CHILDREN OF THE FIELDS

You who spend your waking hours
in the joys of honest toil and ask the world for untormented love,
day after day deplete your strength, and the night, benevolent,
nurturing, is your sentry, and with the day you burst forth whole
    again.

Fertile greens. Your children are like small human shadows: the
    chains
that from your limited existence you fling
—pure and nude perhaps upon an unseen mountain's side—toward
    tomorrow.
Oh ignorant beings, wise in ways of living, like children of the sun
    you populate the day!

Muscular, vegetal, as weighty as the oak, tenacious as the plow that
    is guided by your hand,
with love, not cruelty, you scratch the earth that in its tender flesh
    sustains you.
And on your brow you have the mark, intense and raw, of the sun's
daily kiss that ripens you till you are dark and sweet,
like the earth herself on whom, once fulfilled, you outstretched your
    body one night.

I see you as the deepest truth,
modest and unique inhabitants of the world,
the ultimate expression of this noble crust,
through which the earth can still speak in words.

Contra el monte que un lujo primaveral hoy lanza, cubriéndose de
  temporal alegría,
destaca el ocre áspero de vuestro cuerpo cierto,
oh permanentes hijos de la tierra crasa,
donde lentos os movéis, seguros como la roca misma de la gleba.

Dejad que, también, un hijo de la espuma que bate el tranquilo
  espesor del mundo firme,
pase por vuestro lado, ligero como ese río
que nace de la nieve instantánea y va a morir al mar,
al mar perpetuo, padre de vida, muerte sola
que esta espumeante voz sin figura cierta espera.

¡Oh destino sagrado! Acaso todavía
el río atraviese ciudades solas,
o ciudades pobladas. Aldeas laboriosas,
o vacíos fantasmas de habitaciones muertas:
tierra, tierra por siempre.

Pero vosotros sois, continuos,
esa certeza única de unos ojos fugaces.

Against the mountain that today displays a spectacle of spring
    covered by its short-lived happiness,
the bitter ochre of your certain body stands out,
oh timeless children of the dense, thick earth,
on which you slowly move, as sound and sure as rock is of the sod.

Permit him, too, a child of the foamy surf, which beats against the
    tranquil thickness of the solid world,
to pass close by your side, as rapid as a river
born of the sudden snow that flows to the sea to die,
to the timeless sea, life's father, the only death
this foaming voice without determined form awaits.

Oh sacred destiny! Perhaps the river
still passes by lonely cities
or peopled ones. Hardworking hamlets,
or the empty phantoms of lifeless habitats:
earth, forever earth.

But you, unceasing, are
that only certainty of transitory eyes.

ÚLTIMO AMOR

¿Quién eres, dime? ¿Amarga sombra
o imagen de la luz? ¿Brilla en tus ojos
una espada nocturna,
cuchilla temerosa donde está mi destino,
o miro dulce en tu mirada el claro
azul del agua en las montañas puras,
lago feliz sin nubes en el seno
que un águila solar copia extendida?

¿Quién eres, quién? Te amé, te amé naciendo.
Para tu lumbre estoy, para ti vivo.
Miro tu frente sosegada, excelsa.
Abre tus ojos, dame, dame vida.
Sorba en su llama tenebrosa el sino
que me devora, el hambre de tus venas.
Sorba su fuego derretido y sufra,
sufra por ti, por tu carbón prendiéndome.
Sólo soy tuyo si en mis venas corre
tu lumbre sola, si en mis pulsos late
un ascua, otra ascua: sucesión de besos.
Amor, amor, tu ciega pesadumbre,
tu fulgurante gloria me destruye,
lucero solo, cuerpo inscrito arriba,
que ardiendo puro se consuma a solas.

Pero besarte, niña mía, ¿es muerte?
¿Es sólo muerte tu mirada? ¿Es ángel,

FINAL LOVE

Who are you, tell me? A bitter shadow
or an image of the light? Does a sword of night
gleam in your eyes,
a fearful knife on which my destiny now lies,
or do I in your gentle look behold the limpid
blue of waters in the mountain's purity,
the happy cloudless lake in whose bosom
a solar eagle copies wings outspread.

Who are you, who? I loved you, loved you from birth.
For your brilliance I exist, for you I live.
I behold your brow, untroubled and sublime.
Open your eyes and give me, give me life.
Absorb in its dark flame the destiny
that is devouring me, the hunger of your veins.
Absorb its melted fire and suffer,
suffer through you and ignite me with your blazing coal.
I am yours alone if in my veins there runs
your own prodigious light, if in my pulse there throbs
an ember, another ember: a sequence of kisses.
Love, love, your blind sorrow,
your shining glory overwhelms me,
lonely star, body inscribed above,
that in the pureness of its flame consumes itself.

But does kissing you, child of mine, mean death?
Is your glance only death? Is it an angel

o es una espada larga que me clava
contra los cielos, mientras fuljo sangres
y acabo en luz, en titilante estrella?

Niña de amor, tus rayos inocentes,
tu pelo terso, tus paganos brillos,
tu carne dulce que a mi lado vive,
no sé, no sé, no sabré nunca, nunca,
si es sólo amor, si es crimen, si es mi muerte.

Golfo sombrío, vórtice, te supe,
te supe siempre. En lágrimas te beso,
paloma niña, cándida tibieza,
pluma feliz: tus ojos me aseguran
que el cielo sigue azul, que existe el agua,
y en tus labios la pura luz crepita
toda contra mi boca amaneciendo.

¿Entonces? Hoy, frente a tus ojos miro,
miro mi enigma. Acerco ahora a tus labios
estos labios pasados por el mundo,
y temo, y sufro y beso. Tibios se abren
los tuyos, y su brillo sabe a soles
jóvenes, a reciente luz, a auroras.

or a lengthy sword that nails me
against the sky, my blood gleaming,
and I perish in the light, in a twinkling star?

Child of love, your innocent beams,
your shining hair, your pagan gleams,
your tender flesh that lives here by my side,
I do not know, I do not know, will never, never know
if this is only love, is a crime, is my death.

Somber gulf and vortex, I knew you,
knew you always. With tears I kiss you,
dovelike child, white and warm,
happy plumage: your eyes assure me that
the sky is ever blue, that water exists,
and on your lips the pure light dawning
sizzles against my mouth.

And now? Today I look into your eyes
and see a mystery. Now I approach your lips,
those that have crossed the world,
and I fear, I suffer and kiss. Your warm lips open,
and their brilliance smacks of youthful suns,
of newborn light and of the break of day.

¿Entonces? Negro brilla aquí tu pelo,
onda de noche. En él hundo mi boca.
¡Qué sabor a tristeza, qué presagio
infinito de soledad! Lo sé: algún día
estaré solo. Su perfume embriaga
de sombría certeza, lumbre pura,
tenebrosa belleza inmarcesible,
noche cerrada y tensa en que mis labios
fulgen como una luna ensangrentada.

¡Pero no importa! Gire el mundo y dame,
dame tu amor, y muera yo en la ciencia
fútil, mientras besándote rodamos
por el espacio y una estrella se alza.

And now? Black shines your hair,
the waxing tide of night. I plunge my mouth into it.
What bitter taste of sadness, what infinite
presentiment of solitude! I know: one day
I'll be alone. Its scent intoxicates
with somber certainty, pure light,
tenebrious undying beauty,
dark taut night in which my lips
glow like a bloodstained moon.

But no matter! Let the world spin on, and give me,
give me your love, and let me in futile
knowledge die, as kissing you we wheel
through space, and a star ascends.

AL CIELO

El puro azul ennoblece
mi corazón. Sólo tú, ámbito altísimo
inaccesible a mis labios, das paz y calma plenas
al agitado corazón con que estos años vivo.
Reciente la historia de mi juventud, alegre todavía
y dolorosa ya, mi sangre se agita, recorre su cárcel
y, roja de oscura hermosura, asalta el muro
débil del pecho, pidiendo tu vista,
cielo feliz que en la mañana rutilas,
que asciendes entero y majestuoso presides
mi frente clara, donde mis ojos te besan.
Luego declinas, oh sereno, oh puro don de la altura,
cielo intocable que siempre me pides, sin cansancio, mis besos,
como de cada mortal, virginal, solicitas.
Sólo por ti mi frente pervive al sucio embate de la sangre.
Interiormente combatido de la presencia dolorida y feroz,
recuerdo impío de tanto amor y de tanta belleza,
una larga espada tendida como sangre recorre
mis venas, y sólo tú, cielo agreste, intocado,
das calma a este acero sin tregua que me yergue en el mundo.

Baja, baja dulce para mí y da paz a mi vida.
Hazte blando a mi frente como una mano tangible
y oiga yo como un trueno que sea dulce una voz
que, azul, sin celajes, clame largamente en mi cabellera.
Hundido en ti, besado del azul poderoso y materno,

TO THE SKY

Pure azure elevates
my heart. Only you, highest expanse,
ever beyond my lips, give utter peace and calm
to the anguished heart I have lived with these past years.
The story of my youth a recent one, happy yet
already pained, my blood stirs, races in its jail
and, red with dark beauty, attacks the weak
rampart of my chest, pleading for the sight of you,
joyous sky who sparkles in the morning,
who ascends entire to reign majestically
over my shining countenance, as my eyes kiss you.
Then you descend, oh serene, pure gift from above,
ever beyond my reach, beseeching me untiringly for kisses,
as you request of every mortal, as though virgins all.
Through you alone my head survives blood's depraved assault.
Assailed within myself by a grievous and ferocious presence,
unholy memory of so much love and so much beauty,
a long flat sword like blood runs through
my veins, and only you, bucolic sky, untouched,
can calm this unrelenting steel that holds me upright in the world.

Descend with gentleness, descend for me and give peace to my life.
Be like a loving hand that softly strokes my brow,
let me hear, like a gentle thunderclap, a voice,
blue cloudless voice crying out inside my head.
Engulfed by you, kissed by your strong maternal blue,

mis labios sumidos en tu celeste luz apurada
sientan tu roce meridiano, y mis ojos
ebrios de tu estelar pensamiento te amen,
mientras así peinado suavemente por el soplo de los astros,
mis oídos escuchan al único amor que no muere.

let my lips plunge into your pure celestial light
to feel your meridian touch, let my eyes,
drunk with your starry thought, love you,
and my hair gently combed by a breath from the stars,
and my ears listen to the only love that does not die.

LA ISLA

Isla gozosa que lentamente posada
sobre la mar instable
navegas silenciosa por un mundo ofrecido.
En tu seno me llevas, ¿rumbo al amor? No hay sombras.
¿En qué entrevista playa un fantasma querido
me espera siempre a solas, tenaz, tenaz, sin dueño?
Olas sin paz que eternamente jóvenes
aquí rodáis hasta mis pies intactos.
Miradme vuestro, mientras gritáis hermosas
con espumosa lengua que eterna resucita.
Yo os amo. Allá una vela no es un suspiro leve.
Oh, no mintáis, dejadme en vuestros gozos.
Alzad un cuerpo riente, una amenaza
de amor, que se deshaga rompiente entre mis brazos.
Cantad tendidamente sobre la arena vívida
y ofrezca el sol su duro beso ardiente
sobre los cuerpos jóvenes, continuos, derramados.

Mi cuerpo está desnudo entre desnudos. Grito
con vuestra desnudez no humana entre mis labios.
Recorra yo la espuma con insaciable boca,
mientras las rocas duran, hermosas allá al fondo.
No son barcos humanos los humos pensativos
que una sospecha triste del hombre allá descubren.
¡Oh, no!: ¡el cielo te acepta, trazo ligero y bueno
que un ave nunca herida sobre el azul dejara!

THE ISLAND

Joyous island languorously poised
above the changing sea,
you sail in silence through a proffered world.
You carry me within your breast, toward love? There are no
    shadows.
On what half-seen shore does a beloved apparition—
always alone, fierce, fierce, possessed by no one—wait for me?
Waves never at peace and ever young,
here you swirl about, yet never touch, my feet.
Look, I am yours, as your beauty cries out
with frothy tongue eternally reborn.
I love you. There a sail is not a fragile sigh.
Oh, don't delude me, leave me in your delights.
Lift up a laughing body, threat
of love, that dissolves in tidal swells between my arms.
Waves stretched along the gleaming sand,
you sing and the sun bestows its hard burning kiss
upon young bodies ever overflowing.

My body, naked among the naked. I cry out,
your nonhuman nakedness between my lips.
Let me traverse the surf with insatiable mouth,
as long as rocks endure, in all their distant beauty.
They are not human vessels, those pensive fumes
that discover a sad suspicion of man.
Oh no! The sky accepts you, frail and fitting trace
that a gull unwounded may have left upon the blue!

Fanstasma, dueño mío, si un viento hinche tus sábanas,
tu nube en la rompiente febril, sabe que existen
cuerpos de amor que eternos irrumpen, se deshacen . . .,
acaban, resucitan. Yo canto con sus lenguas.

Apparition, my master, if a wind swells your sheets,
your cloud on the fevered shoal, it knows about
love's bodies that eternally erupt, disintegrate . . .,
die, resuscitate. I sing with their tongues.

NO BASTA

Pero no basta, no, no basta
la luz del sol, ni su cálido aliento.
No basta el misterio oscuro de una mirada.
Apenas bastó un día el rumoroso fuego de los bosques.
Supe del mar. Pero tampoco basta.

En medio de la vida, al filo de las mismas estrellas,
mordientes, siempre dulces en sus bordes inquietos,
sentí iluminarse mi frente.
No era tristeza, no. Triste es el mundo;
pero la inmensa alegría invasora del universo
reinó también en los pálidos días.

No era tristeza. Un mensaje remoto
de una invisible luz modulaba unos labios
aéreamente, sobre pálidas ondas,
ondas de un mar intangible a mis manos.

Una nube con peso, nube cargada acaso de pensamiento estelar,
se detenía sobre las aguas, pasajera en la tierra,
quizá envío celeste de universos lejanos
que un momento detiene su paso por el éter.

Yo vi dibujarse una frente,
frente divina: hendida de una arruga luminosa,

NOT ENOUGH

Not enough, no, not enough
the sunlight nor its warm breath.
The uncertain mystery of a glance—not enough.
The rustling fire in the woods one day—hardly enough.
I learned about the sea. Even that is not enough.

Halfway through my life, near the very stars,
their restless edges jagged but ever gentle,
I felt their light on my face.
It was not sadness, no. The world is sad;
but the vast invading joy of the universe
reigned even on the grayest days.

It was not sadness. The distant message
of an unseen light harmonized the lips
from high above, above the pale waves,
waves in a sea beyond my hands' reach.

A heavy cloud, perhaps laden with starry thoughts,
paused above the water, transient on earth,
perhaps a celestial envoy from distant universes
pausing briefly in its passage through the ether.

I saw a face taking shape,
a godlike face: furrowed by a shining fold.

atravesó un instante preñada de un pensamiento sombrío.
Vi por ella cruzar un relámpago morado, vi unos ojos
cargados de infinita pesadumbre brillar,
y vi a la nube alejarse, densa, oscura, cerrada,
silenciosa, hacia el meditabundo ocaso sin barreras.

El cielo alto quedó como vacío.
Mi grito resonó en la oquedad sin bóveda
y se perdió, como mi pensamiento que voló deshaciéndose,
como un llanto hacia arriba, al vacío desolador, al hueco.

Sobre la tierra mi bulto cayó. Los cielos eran
sólo conciencia mía, soledad absoluta.
Un vacío de Dios sentí sobre mi carne,
y sin mirar arriba, nunca, nunca, hundí mi frente en la arena
y besé sólo a la tierra, a la oscura, sola,
desesperada tierra que me acogía.

Así sollocé sobre el mundo.
¡Qué luz lívida, qué espectral vacío velador,
qué ausencia de Dios sobre mi cabeza derribada
vigilaba sin límites mi cuerpo convulso?
¡Oh madre, madre, sólo en tus brazos siento
mi miseria! Sólo en tu seno martirizado por mi llanto
rindo mi bulto, sólo en ti me deshago.

an instant pregnant with a somber thought passed overhead.
I saw the purple lightning streak across it, saw eyes
gleaming, heavy with infinite grief,
and saw the dense, dark, stormy, silent cloud
recede untrammeled toward the pensive setting sun.

The upper reach of sky remained empty.
My cry resounded in the domeless void
and was lost, like my thoughts that dissolved in flight,
like a lament to the heavens, to the desolate void, the empty hole.

The weight of my body fell to the earth. The heavens were
nothing but my consciousness, an utter solitude.
On my flesh I felt God's absence,
and without an upward glance, never, never, I buried my face in the
    sand
and kissed the empty earth, the somber, lonely,
despairing earth that gave me refuge.

And so I wept over the world.
What purplish light, what watchful spectral emptiness,
what absence of God above my battered head
kept endless vigil on my convulsing body?
Oh mother, mother, only in your arms do I feel
my misery! Only on your bosom martyred by my lament
can I yield my body's weight, only in you do I dissolve.

Estos límites que me oprimen,
esta arcilla que de la mar naciera,
que aquí quedó en tus playas,
hija tuya, obra tuya, luz tuya,
extinguida te pide su confusión gloriosa,
te pide sólo a ti, madre inviolada,
madre mía de tinieblas calientes,
seno sólo donde el vacío reina,
mi amor, mi amor, hecho ya tú, hecho tú sólo.

Todavía quisiera, madre,
con mi cabeza apoyada en tu regazo,
volver mi frente hacia el cielo
y mirar hacia arriba, hacia la luz, hacia la luz pura,
y sintiendo tu calor, echado dulcemente sobre tu falda,
contemplar el azul, la esperanza risueña,
la promesa de Dios, la presentida frente amorosa.
¡Qué bien desde ti, sobre tu caliente carne robusta,
mirar las ondas puras de la divinidad bienhechora!
¡Ver la luz amanecer por oriente, y entre la aborrascada nube preñada
contemplar un instante la purísima frente divina destellar,
y esos inmensos ojos bienhechores
donde el mundo alzado quiere entero copiarse
y mecerse en un vaivén de mar, de estelar mar entero,
compendiador de estrellas, de luceros, de soles,

Those limits that oppress me,
this clay born of the sea,
that remained here on your shores,
your child, your creation and your light,
lifeless clay asks you for its glorious disorder,
asks of you alone, chaste mother,
mother mine of warm shadows,
solitary breast where the void reigns,
my love, my love, become now you, only you.

Still I would wish, mother,
with my head upon your lap,
to turn my face toward the sky,
and look upward toward the light, toward your pure light,
and feeling your warmth as I lie gently on your skirt,
to contemplate the blue, the smiling hope,
God's promise, the immanent loving face.
How good, from upon your strong warm flesh
to watch the clear waves of the beneficent deity!
To see the light dawn in the east, and through the storm-filled cloud
to contemplate for an instant the gleams of that purest godhead
and those vast beneficent eyes
in which the risen world longs to be reflected entire,
and to be cradled in the gentle rocking of the sea, of the star-lit sea
    entire,
compendium of stars, of galaxies, of suns,

mientras suena la música universal, hecha ya frente pura,
radioso amor, luz bella, felicidad sin bordes!

Así, madre querida,
tú puedes saber bien —lo sabes, siento tu beso secreto de sabiduría—
que el mar no baste, que no basten los bosques,
que una mirada oscura llena de humano misterio,
no baste; que no baste, madre, el amor,
como no baste el mundo.

Madre, madre, sobre tu seno hermoso
echado tiernamente, déjame así decirte
mi secreto; mira mi lágrima
besarte; madre que todavía me sustentas,
madre cuya profunda sabiduría me sostiene ofrecido.

while the music of the universe sounds, transformed into a face of
    piety,
radiant love, lovely light, happiness without end!

Thus, beloved mother,
you may well know—yes, you know, for I feel your secret kiss of
    wisdom—
that the sea is not enough, forests are not enough,
a somber glance imbued with human mystery
is not enough; that love itself is not enough, mother,
nor is the world.

Mother, mother, against your lovely breast
gently cradled, now let me share my secret
with you; watch as my tear
gives you a kiss; mother who sustains me still,
mother whose deepest wisdom sustains my very self.

Designer: Steve Renick
Compositor: Editorial Excelsior
Printer: Edwards Brothers, Inc.
Binder: Edwards Brothers, Inc.
Text: 10/14 Bembo
Display: Bembo